I 011.002
2nd copy

VGM Opportunities Series

OPPORTUNITIES IN LASER TECHNOLOGY CAREERS

Jan Bone

Revised Edition

Foreword by
Ted Maiman
Inventor of the first laser

VGM Career Horizons
NTC/Contemporary Publishing Group

Library of Congress Cataloging-in-Publication Data

Bone, Jan
    Opportunities in laser technology careers / Jan Bone ; revised by Julie Rigby ;
foreward by Ted Marman.—Rev. ed.
      p. ; cm. (VGM opportunities series)
    Includes bibliographical references.
    ISBN 0-658-00203-1 (cloth)—ISBN 0-658-00204-X (paper)
      1. Laser industry—Vocational guidance. I. Rigby, Julie. II. Title.
TA1677 .B66 2000
621.36'6'023—dc21
                                   99-52563
                                        CIP

Cover photograph: © PhotoDisc, Inc.

Published by VGM Career Horizons
A division of NTC/Contemporary Publishing Group, Inc.
4255 West Touhy Avenue, Lincolnwood (Chicago), Illinois 60712-1975 U.S.A.
Copyright © 2000 by NTC/Contemporary Publishing Group, Inc.
Printed in the United States of America
International Standard Book Numbers: 0-658-00203-1 (cloth)
                                    0-658-00204-x (paper)

00 01 02 03 04 05 LB 15 14 13 12 11 10 9 8 7 6 5 4 3 2 1

CONTENTS

About the Author v

Foreword vii

Acknowledgments ix

1. Lasers: An Incredible Light 1

The many uses of lasers. What is a laser? The laser patent
war. The importance of the Gould patents.

2. How Lasers Work 12

Parts of a laser. How lasers amplify light. The race to create
the laser. What "coherence" means. Making the first laser.

3. Lasers in Health Care 24

Lasers used in medicine. Lasers in ophthalmology. Lasers
in obstetrics/gynecology. Lasers in podiatry. Working with
lasers. A laser nurse coordinator. A laser coordinator. Laser
safety officers. Laser educators.

4. Lasers in Manufacturing 43

The advantages of lasers. Types of lasers. Learning
more about lasers in manufacturing. Kinds of jobs. Job
descriptions. A laser machinist. Limitations of lasers.

5. Lasers in Military and Space Applications 63

The Strategic Defense Initiative (SDI). The Ballistic Missile
Defense Organization (BMDO). Laser defense and weaponry.

Jobs in military programs. Measurements in space. Lasers on the moon. Jobs with lasers and space.

6. Lasers in Communications................................. **72**

Bell Laboratories. Optical networking. Lasers and optical storage. Hewlett-Packard LaserJet Printers. A press relations coordinator. Holograms. A holography artist.

7. Lasers in Research **87**

Technology transfer. Medical free-electron laser program. Other spin-off applications. Laser fusion. Laser isotope separation. Contract research. Laser research at Battelle. Jobs in research. Security clearance. A laser research scientist.

8. Preparing for a Career in Laser Technologies **98**

Science literacy. College and beyond. University of Rochester. University of Arizona. University of Central Florida.

9. Job Hunting Strategies........................... **112**

Personal characteristics. Be selective about your training. On-line resources. Resumes. Salaries.

10. Women and Minorities........................... **120**

Enrollment statistics. Concentrate on science and math. Society of Women Engineers. American Council on Education.

11. International Opportunities..................... **125**

Laser technology in Canada. Laser technology in Britain. Laser technology in Australia.

Appendix A: Associations **133**

Appendix B: Recommended Reading and Resources..... **142**

ABOUT THE AUTHOR

Jan Bone has been writing professionally for more than forty years, ever since, as a sixteen-year-old, she had her first newspaper job on the Williamsport, Pennsylvania, *Sun*. Her bachelor's degree is from Cornell University, and she holds an M.B.A. degree from Roosevelt University.

When Ted Maiman successfully invented the first working laser in his laboratory at Hughes Aircraft Corporation, Jan was busy caring for four sons—the oldest in kindergarten. During the three decades that followed, however, her interest in technology has grown significantly.

From 1977 to 1985 Jan served as an elected member of the Board of Trustees of William Rainey Harper College in Palatine, Illinois, and from 1979 to 1985 she was board secretary. During that time, the college set up a CAD/CAM center to train students and professionals in computer-aided design and computer-aided manufacturing, sparking her interest in the field.

She has studied production management and is an associate member of the Society of Manufacturing Engineers and two of its divisions: Computer and Automated Systems Association (CASA) and Robotics International (RI). Because of her interest in lasers and laser technology, she is also a member of SME's Laser Council.

A prolific freelance writer, Jan is senior writer for the *Chicago Tribune*'s special advertising sections and has written special features sections material for the *Chicago Sun-Times* since 1982. She has written for publications as diverse as *Bank Marketing,*

Family Circle, Woman's World, Medical Tribune, and *National ENQUIRER.* In 1988 she was named contributing editor of *Bank Administration,* the magazine of bank management. Jan is also a part-time writing instructor at Roosevelt University in Chicago.

She is coauthor with Ron Johnson of *Understanding the Film* (NTC/Contemporary Publishing Group, Inc., Lincolnwood, Illinois, 1998, 5th edition) and author of *Opportunities in Film Careers, Opportunities in Cable Television, Opportunities in Telecommunications, Opportunities in Computer-Aided Design and Computer-Aided Manufacturing,* and *Opportunities in Robotics Careers* in the VGM Career Horizons series.

Jan has won the Chicago Working Newsman's Scholarship, the Illinois Education School Bell Award for Best Comprehensive Coverage of Education by dailies under 250,000 circulation, and an American Political Science Award for Distinguished Reporting of Public Affairs. Since 1983, she has been listed in *Who's Who of American Women.*

She is widowed, the mother of four married sons, and the grand-mother of four.

FOREWORD

It takes courage to work on something new and different—not to be part of the majority of people who are comfortable doing things in a familiar pattern. When I made the first laser in 1960, I found out firsthand how satisfying it can be to stay with an idea you believe in.

From the public relations standpoint, the press announcement of that laser was extraordinarily successful. The news hit the front page of every major newspaper in the United States and of many papers overseas. Unfortunately, a typical headline read, "Los Angeles Man Discovers Science Fiction Death Ray!"

Shortly thereafter, the owner of Knotts Berry Farm, a popular amusement park, phoned. He wanted to use the laser in a shoot-the-duck game. A representative of the Ice Capades wanted laser light for the spotlights on his performers because of its purity. The president of the American Meat Packers Association wanted to use a laser to stun hogs.

Here were three forward-thinking, progressive, entrepreneurial people who looked on lasers as a tool they could use creatively in their work. Whether it was feasible or not was beside the point. They were ready to try.

Nearly forty years later, the laser is still as exciting and marvelous as it was in its "gee whiz!" days. I'm no longer pulled aside at scientific conferences and asked, "Do you think the laser is ever really going to be useful?" Instead, when someone reads my name badge, they may say, "My grandmother's eyesight was saved because of laser surgery," or even, "Thank you for my job."

The acceptance of lasers came rather slowly, just like that of the airplane and the auto. I seriously doubt that the Wright brothers ever dreamed there would be flights around the world and planes carrying hundreds of passengers. And for many years, automobiles were looked on as a rich man's toy.

I certainly didn't envision lasers becoming part of everyday life... as familiar as the supermarket checkout scanner or the compact audiodisc.

From the beginning, I thought lasers could be used in medicine, but I didn't dream how fantastic today's results would be or the difference they would make in diagnosis and surgery. I felt lasers would be used in communication, but I didn't really see how. It wasn't practical until low-loss fiber was invented ten years later.

Today, lasers in manufacturing improve yield and productivity. You can cut through half an inch of steel with a laser faster than just about any other way.

Today, lasers are used for computer printers and extremely high-density information storage. And tomorrow, tiny lasers inside a computer will achieve much faster speed and performance with optical computing than digital computers now offer.

It's even conceivable that lasers could be the key to solving the energy problem through laser fusion!

To me, lasers are one of the fastest growth industries in the world. There will be jobs in laser technology, not only in working with current laser applications, but also jobs that don't yet exist. The courage of young people—people like yourself who are not afraid to go ahead with ideas they believe in, despite possible discouragement—will make those jobs possible.

Books such as this, which help introduce young people to lasers, play an important role in stimulating imagination and creativity. I hope the laser brings as much satisfaction to your life as it has to mine.

Ted Maiman
Inventor of the first laser

ACKNOWLEDGMENTS

The following individuals were especially helpful in the development of this book: Gary Benedict, Edesly Canto, Patrick Doolan, Ellet Drake, Jack Dyer, Robert Ford, Gordon Gould, Susan Hicks, Joe Hlubucek, Reena Jabamoni, Rick Jackson, Frank Jacoby, Tung H. Jeong, James Johnson, Alan J. Jones, Hamid Madjid, Fortuneé Massuda, Vivian Merchant, George L. Paul, Jeri Peterson, Judith Pfister, Robert Prycz, Greg Rixon, Howard Rudzinsky, John Ruselowski, George Sanborn, Fred Seaman, M. J. Soileau, Doris Vila, and Carol Worth.

Special thanks to Theodore H. Maiman.

The author also acknowledges the assistance of the ABET, Alberta Laser Centre, American Association of Engineering Societies, American Society for Laser Medicine and Surgery, Australian Embassy, Battelle Laboratories, Bell Labs, British Information Service, Edison Foundation, Electronic Engineering Associates, Gas Research Institute, Hewlett-Packard, Institute of Industrial Engineers, Lake Forest College, Laser Focus/Electro-Optics, Laser Institute of America, Lawrence Livermore National Laboratories, Optical Society of America, Raycon Corporation, School of the Art Institute of Chicago, Society of Manufacturing Engineers, Society of Women Engineers, SPIE, University of Arizona Optical Sciences Center, University of Central Florida/CREOL, University of Rochester Institute of Optics, and Westinghouse.

CHAPTER 1

LASERS: AN INCREDIBLE LIGHT

When laser expert M. J. Soileau visits fourth grade classrooms, he brings a laser with him. The small black box, about eight inches long and one and a half inches wide, intrigues the youngsters, who crowd around him asking what it is. But when Soileau tells them that this simple box is a laser, they don't believe him.

"How come you can't see the beam?" they ask. To them, the word "lasers" conjures up images of the lightsticks used by the Jedi warriors in the *Star Wars* movies, not this ordinary-looking black box.

Soileau, who heads University of Central Florida's CREOL, the Center for Research and Education in Optics and Lasers, is unfazed by their question. He is accustomed to people of all ages not really understanding what lasers are and the many ways that they are used in real life. He explains to the students that light doesn't show up in an unpolluted atmosphere. To see the beam, he explains, all he needs to do is clap two blackboard erasers together, making chalk fly through the air. A light beam aimed through the dust cloud will then be noticeable.

The second question Soileau invariably gets from a grade school class—as well as from most adults!—is, "Don't lasers make holes in things?" He explains that lasers can make holes and are used for precisely that reason in many industrial and medical applications. However, many lasers aren't powerful enough to do anything more than appear bright.

Although most of us don't truly understand lasers and what they can be used for, they nevertheless fascinate and amaze us. When we think of lasers, we imagine powerful bursts of light, intense levels of heat, and very advanced technology. Lasers are all that, and more. Developed just over thirty years ago, lasers have radically changed industry, medicine, and science. Without our even being aware of it, lasers have entered almost every aspect of our daily lives.

THE MANY USES OF LASERS

The most common lasers are used to transmit and store information. When we listen to music on our compact disc player, we are utilizing the power of lasers. The sound is recorded by a laser beam, which burns a pattern of dots onto a compact disc. Then a tiny semiconductor laser in our CD player reads those dots and converts them back into sound. Since only the light from the laser touches the CD, you hear a very clean and clear sound, without the scratches and dust that you would hear on an old vinyl record.

Just as CD players have replaced other methods of recording music, the process of recording information on discs via lasers has revolutionized libraries and other warehouses of information. Lasers are used to create the compact discs that store databases, encyclopedias, art, and all the other kinds of information you regularly access by computer.

And after we have used a CD-ROM disc and found the information we need for a school report, lasers are at work when we print up that report. Laser printers print quickly, creating pages that look as if they were printed professionally. The scanning laser within the printer moves across a light-drum, which attracts ink where the laser has hit it and transfers the ink to the paper as it rolls by.

The scanning laser also is used to read as well as to write. Every time you buy groceries at a supermarket, compact discs at a music store, or clothing at a department store, the scanner reads the labels with the Universal Product Codes' striped patterns and rings up the price.

Or, let's say you wanted to call up some friends and invite them to a laser light show. The fiber-optic cables used by most telephone companies use tiny semiconductor lasers to carry your call across town or around the world. The sound of your voice is converted to electrical pulses and then converted to laser light that can travel through the fiber-optic cables. Using lasers to carry telephone calls is far more efficient than the traditional technology used in telephones, which sent calls over copper wires. Because lasers can pulse very rapidly, one miniscule glass fiber, no wider than a human hair, can actually transmit the calls of more than twenty-thousand old-fashioned copper wires!

Factories use lasers to manufacture an astonishing array of products and materials. Lasers can be powerful enough to cut through more than an inch of a strong metal such as steel, and they can be precise enough to drill two-hundred holes on the head of a pin. Lasers also are used to weld metal, solder tiny circuits for electronics parts, drill miniscule holes, and cut cloth for clothing.

Scientists have discovered that lasers provide a much more accurate way of taking measurements. Using lasers, we now can calculate the distance to the moon much more precisely than ever before. In 1969, astronauts placed an object on the moon that can reflect back a laser beam to its corresponding system on Earth. Lasers are used by the military to guide "smart bombs," transmit messages on the battlefield, and for training to simulate the explosiveness of real ammunition. And just as we have found military uses for lasers, we also are cured by lasers. Doctors in almost every specialty use lasers for a host of procedures, including mending tissue, correcting vision problems, and even erasing lines and wrinkles!

From tiny lasers like the one in a laser pointer to the world's biggest laser, which is housed in a building about the size of an NBA basketball arena at California's Lawrence Livermore National Laboratory, lasers have taken a place in our world. It's hard to imagine that the first working laser was not even invented until 1960. The old saying was that lasers were "a solution in search of a problem." Unlike most inventions, which are created to address a specific need or problem, lasers were developed before there were any practical applications for it. Now lasers are dependable and ubiquitous enough that it is hard to imagine our world without them. And the possibilities for laser use keep growing, as new applications are continuously being developed.

WHAT IS A LASER?

The word *laser* itself is an acronym—*l*ight *a*mplification by *s*timulated *e*mission of *r*adiation. Radiation in this sense is another word for electromagnetic energy, which includes light. A laser is a device that generates or amplifies coherent radiation at frequencies in the infrared, visible, or ultraviolet regions of the electromagnetic spectrum.

Laser light has several properties that make it different from regular light. First, it is often "collimated"—meaning that it travels for long distances in a narrow beam, rather than fragmenting off in many directions as regular light does. Lasers can produce short bursts of light, or they can be used to create a continuous beam. Because it can focus narrowly, the light from a laser can be much more intense than regular light, especially in bursts. The power from a laser beam can be everything from just a few microwatts to several billion watts in short bursts.

Laser light is also coherent. The light waves stay synchronized over long distances. And it is only one color, making it monochromatic. Some laser beams are even invisible, as they produce light in the infrared or ultraviolet wavelengths.

Lasers involve complex terminology and science, and it is natural to be confused by the physics and technology of this intricate invention. Chapter 2 explains how lasers work and tells the story of how Theodore H. Maiman invented the laser in 1960, while he was a research scientist at Hughes Aircraft. Maiman calculates that the whole nine-month project that resulted in the first operating laser cost Hughes no more than $50,000, including his salary, his assistant's salary, and overhead. That is certainly a bargain when you consider that the worldwide market for diode lasers alone reached $2.15 billion in 1998!

In subsequent chapters you will discover the exciting array of opportunities available to people who want to work in the fast-growing field of laser technology. Only a few years ago, lasers were so exotic that they were the exclusive domain of Ph.D.s and other advanced scientists. Now lasers represent a multibillion dollar industry, and we encounter lasers in nearly every aspect of our lives. There are even manuals for building lasers at home! Truly, the opportunities for an exciting career in laser technology are limitless.

THE LASER PATENT WAR

A controversy over patent rights is one of the more fascinating aspects of the early years of the laser. Indeed, this patent "war," which began in 1957 in the physics department at Columbia University, raged for more than thirty years and caused many divisions within the laser world. The battle was over who first had the idea for the laser. Was it Dr. Charles H. Townes, a physics professor at Columbia, and Arther L. Schawlow, his brother-in-law and research partner at Bell Laboratories? Or was it Gordon Gould, who was a thirty-seven-year-old graduate student at Columbia?

In 1987, three decades after the controversy began, Gould won an important legal victory when he was awarded the patent covering gas discharge lasers. Gas discharge lasers are used in roughly 60 percent of all commercial lasers, so this was an important financial victory for Gould as well.

"I conceived the laser in late 1957," Gould remembers, "and I should have applied for a patent right away, but I thought (wrongly, as it turned out) that I had to have a working model first. I left Columbia University, where I was a graduate student, and joined a company where I thought I could get a laser built. Although I applied for a patent in April 1959, by that time there were other inventors applying for patents on various aspects of lasers."

As Gould explains, the U.S. Patent Office has a procedure for deciding who has the right to a patent where claims overlap in applications—a situation the Patent Office calls "interference."

"My application contained many inventions, including two different types of lasers, and it covered various other aspects of lasers. Consequently, there were five interferences with other inventors."

One of those inventors was Charles Townes. In 1951 Townes, continuing experiments first begun in Germany by other researchers, suggested separating a beam of ammonia molecules into two portions. The molecules in each portion of the beam did not have the same energy states; in one portion, the energy state would be higher. Early scientists studying quantum mechanics, a particular branch of physics, had previously believed that if an electromagnetic beam with a particular resonant frequency were passed through a medium, molecules of the beam in a higher state of energy might be stimulated to fall to a lower state of energy—and in the process might reinforce the primary beam.

Townes used a microwave oscillator in his experiments and passed the high-energy portion of his ammonia beam through a cavity that resonated at the frequency that matched the energy difference between the high- and low-energy states. Eventually Townes was awarded a patent for his *maser,* a word coined as an acronym for *m*icrowave *a*mplification by *s*timulated *e*mission of *r*adiation. Masers and lasers are theoretically similar, but masers operate at frequencies in the microwave region of the spectrum, while lasers operate in the light range of the spectrum. Later on, the Townes patent was licensed to laser manufacturers.

Meanwhile, at Bell Laboratories Arthur Schawlow was continuing research on optical masers. Together, Schawlow and Townes proposed a way to get optical maser action. Their plan called for an alkaline vapor to be placed in an optical cavity to serve as an active medium. Such a medium, they thought, could be excited in such a way that if an optical wave were present, it would be amplified as it moved through the medium. According to Gould, Schawlow and Townes didn't realize the active medium could be excited by light.

The work of Townes and Schawlow eventually led to the awarding of another patent in 1960, U.S. Patent Number 2,929,922. Because Schawlow and Townes had applied for a patent before Gould's original application, they were considered the "senior parties."

"I was unable to prove the diligence required to establish a date for my work that was earlier than their patent application," Gould says. "They thought they had won." What the Schawlow and Townes patent claimed to cover, Gould says, was the resonator—the pair of mirrors required to shine the light back and forth through the laser amplifier.

In 1964, Townes won the Nobel prize in physics for developing the laser and maser. And so it seemed that the issue had been settled. Gould, however, had by no means given up his fight to be recognized for his work with lasers and to have his claims recognized by the U.S. Patent Office. It was a long and difficult struggle. In fact, the Patent Office eventually required Gould to divide his original application into six different applications.

"What took up the time," Gould says, "was dealing with these interferences. Each took several years to resolve. They were run in sequence rather than at the same time, so the determination on the last one was not completed until 1973, fourteen years after I'd originally filed. By that time, the industry had virtually forgotten there was such a thing as the Gould patent applications."

Complicating the matter further was the fact that the laser industry had become large and mature by 1977, the year in which Gould was issued his first patent on amplifiers. By then there were many companies, many laser products, and many ways in which lasers were being used. "The amount of money involved for royalties was big," Gould says, "big enough so that nobody was going to just write me a check if I called them up and told them about my patents."

What Gould's two patents covered were two different kinds of amplifiers that built up the strength of the light beam. One amplifier was the so-called optically pumped laser, consisting of a rod of appropriate material, such as ruby, with a flashlamp beside it. The light from the flashlamp excites the ruby to a state where it serves as an amplifier.

Nearly one-third of all lasers today, Gould says, are optically pumped—making that patent a significant one.

In 1979 Gould was issued a second patent. That patent covered the use of lasers for several different kinds of processes that require heat: welding, heat treating, evaporating materials, and similar chemical reactions.

The third patent issued to Gould, in November 1987, is probably the most important of all. It covers a different kind of amplifier, the discharge laser. When this patent was issued, U.S. Senator Arlen Spector of Pennsylvania held an award ceremony and press conference honoring Gould. Since Senator Spector heads the subcommittee that oversees the U.S. Patent Office, his support and acknowledgment of Gould were significant.

"The awarding of patents was established in the U.S. Constitution," Gould says. "Our forefathers felt there should be a patent system to give an inventor some rights to his invention…to encourage inventors to get the inventions out, instead of holding them secret. Yet it's clear that if it takes twenty-eight years to get a patent issued, the system is not working as intended."

Gould received another laser patent in 1988—a patent he refers to as "the Brewster angle window patent." Some laser tubes have slanted windows on the end. When those windows are at a particular angle (Brewster's angle), laser gas can pass through them without any loss of power. "That's an important development in discharge lasers," Gould explains, "because the gases have to be contained in the laser tube, and you want to get the beam through the tube without any power loss."

Although the CO_2 laser is covered under his 1979 patent for the discharge laser, Gould says that "the more patents you have, the less likely it is that someone will attempt to overturn them."

THE IMPORTANCE OF THE GOULD PATENTS

Since the beginning of the laser industry, the question of who had the rights to license lasers (because they owned the patents) has been controversial. Gould, of course, contended for nearly thirty years that he should be recognized and awarded patents for his work.

Townes was awarded his original patent for masers and won the Nobel prize for his achievements with ammonia maser and subsequent developments in masers and lasers. Schawlow and Townes received a laser patent in March 1960.

Almost immediately after Schawlow and Townes received their patent, Gould precipitated an interference proceeding in the U.S. Patent Office. Although the Patent Office later decided the Schawlow-Townes patent had been properly awarded, the patent expired (as all patents do) seventeen years after it was issued. Gould received his first patent (U.S. Patent Number 4,053,845) for "Optically Pumped Laser Amplifiers" on October 11, 1977.

With patents in hand and with a strong determination to win what he felt was due him, Gould sued various laser companies, charging that they had infringed on his patent rights. It was not an easy legal battle; one of the patent infringement suits dragged on for more than ten years. A significant victory in 1987 against one of the leading laser companies was pivotal since it showed laser companies that even a properly defended suit (Gould's description) was lost. "That verdict showed other companies in the laser industry that my patents were valid," Gould says.

Millions of dollars were at stake in these patents wars, including penalties from laser companies found to be infringing on the Gould patent and royalties from more than two hundred laser manufacturers—royalties that Gould expects to rise to $20 million per year. As a result of winning the "pivotal" suit, Patlex Corporation, which owns a 64 percent interest in the Gould patent, began signing up licensees. With the Gould patents, Patlex holds basic patents covering optically pumped discharge excited laser amplifiers, which are used in 80 percent of the industrial, commercial, and medical applications. In 1992, Patlex merged with AutoFinance Group, a financial-services company. Revenue from laser patents in 1993 were approximately $7 million. The Gould patent on optical pumping expired in 1994, and another applications patent expired in 1996. However, the important discharge-pumping and Brewster-window patents will remain in effect through the early years of the 21st century.

Clearly opportunities in laser technology—jobs you may hold—are related to the financial health of the companies involved with lasers, a health that may hinge on their obligations with respect to the Gould patents. The years ahead will be interesting as these economic and legal questions are resolved.

CHAPTER 2

HOW LASERS WORK

Whether a laser is used to entertain a crowd on the Fourth of July or to perform delicate surgery on a patient's eye, it is operating on the same principle. *L*ight *a*mplification by *s*timulated *e*mission of *r*adiation—laser, that is—indicates a device that generates or amplifies light.

This definition encompasses many different kinds of lasers. Some lasers are solid-state. Others use gases, such as helium and neon (He-Ne), argon, krypton, or carbon dioxide. Ion lasers are used in the printing industry, in light shows, and in therapeutic and diagnostic medicine. Diode (or semiconductor) lasers have proven very valuable in such uses as optical disks and for communications. Indeed, according to a 1999 report in *Laser Focus World,* the worldwide market for diode lasers reached $2.15 billion in 1998, an increase of 17.5 percent over 1997. This was due primarily to the growth in the use of diode lasers in fiberoptic telecommunications. And as more and more people and businesses turn to the Internet, the increased need for fiber-optic networks will surely only increase the demand for diode lasers. Other laser devices include dye lasers and excimer lasers.

PARTS OF A LASER

Lasers generally have four parts: (1) an *active medium* made up of atoms, molecules, ions, or a semiconducting crystal; (2) an *excitation mechanism* that excites the atoms, molecules, ions, or semiconducting crystal into higher energy levels than their normal state; (3) *elements* that let radiation bounce back and forth over and over again through the active medium, amplifying the light; and (4) an *output coupler,* a special mirror at one end of the laser that is constructed in such a way that some of the laser light escapes from the active medium.

One argument used unsuccessfully in a lawsuit about the Gould patent was that laser light occurs in nature. The laser manufacturer suggested that sunlight stimulating the atmosphere of the planet Mars was causing a lasing action. The Martian surface acted as a highly reflective mirror, and the interface between space and the Martian atmosphere acted as an output mirror. Since the components common to all lasers (an energy source, something being lased, and two mirrors) existed as a natural phenomenon, the manufacturer said, lasers should not be patentable. However, the courts did not buy this argument and have upheld the validity of the Gould patents.

"Just about anything can be stimulated," says Gary Benedict, chairman of the Laser Council of the Society of Manufacturing Engineers. "The Americans have made a laser out of Jell-O, and the Russians, out of vodka."

HOW LASERS AMPLIFY LIGHT

Regardless of what active medium is used, however, the purpose of the excitation mechanism is to excite the electrons or ions the medium contains. Scientists think of electrons as traveling around the nucleus of an atom in various orbits. When an electron is excited, the electron jumps to an orbit with a higher energy level. When it returns to the ground state, it gives off energy in the form of a tiny bundle of electromagnetic energy called a photon. If the photon comes near another electron from a different atom—an electron that is in this persistent higher energy state—the photon can induce the premature transition of the second electron so that it, too, gives off a photon. "One photon stimulates the in-step emission of the second photon," explains Dr. Hamid Madjid, associate professor of physics at Pennsylvania State University.

"Each of these two photons can pass another electron and release it, so pretty soon you have four photons, and eight photons, and sixteen photons, and so forth, and you start generating coherent photons.

"This occurs either in a glass tube filled with a mixture of gases, or in a solid material, such as a ruby rod. If those coherent photons move in the axis of the tube or the rod, they induce stimulated emission of more photons.

"On one side of the laser there is a reflecting mirror; on the other, a semitransparent mirror that lets a little light through. The reflecting mirror bounces the small amount of laser light back into the active medium, where it is amplified again and again. This mirror is a special mirror that reflects almost all of the laser light that strikes it. The second mirror, called the output coupler, lets much of the light reflect back into the tube but also lets some of the amplified light escape. This amplified light is called the laser beam."

THE RACE TO CREATE THE LASER

Lasers are so common today that it is even possible to buy the components and build one in your own home. But that was not the case forty years ago.

In 1959, Ted Maiman was a thirty-two-year-old research scientist at Hughes Aircraft Company in Malibu, California. Intrigued by the possibilities, he decided to test for himself the accuracy of measurement by another scientist in a previously published paper in order to see whether a ruby crystal was really as inefficient as had been reported. The maser already existed. Would it be possible to produce something similar, using optical instead of microwave frequencies, to stimulate the emission of radiation and amplify light?

"The race was on," Maiman recalled years later. "Universities and major research labs wanted to be first to make a laser." Among the "players" were Bell Telephone Labs; the Radiation Laboratory at Columbia University; the RCA Labs in Princeton, New Jersey; the Schenectady Research Lab of General Electric; the IBM Labs; and the Lincoln Laboratory of MIT. Meanwhile, other researchers were hard at work in Germany, Japan, and Britain.

Although every scientist was working hard to be "first," Maiman had a somewhat unusual background, a background that he thinks may have been partly responsible for his success in making the first working laser. "What was needed," said Maiman, "was a combination of disciplines and experience."

"I'd gotten my Ph.D. in physics. I was an experimental physicist. I knew the theory and the concepts in physics behind the idea of lasers. I also had practical lab experience, as well as a background in electronics—plus intense motivation and drive."

Maiman's dissertation, completed four years previously, included work in microwaves and optics. He knew about masers and had worked with them, but he believed they wouldn't prove to be practical, since the maser required cooling to within a few degrees of absolute zero. Generating *coherent* light by the concept of stimulated emission sounded more feasible to him.

WHAT "COHERENCE" MEANS

Coherence is one of the unique properties of laser light that makes it so valuable and so important in many laser applications. Coherence can be thought of as an *ordered phenomenon.*

Light from an incandescent bulb, such as an electric light, is incoherent. The light waves coming from that bulb differ from each other in frequency and wavelength, direction, and phase.

These are difficult concepts to understand if you haven't studied physics. Let's talk about them, one at a time.

Scientists believe that light travels in waves, just like waves on the ocean. Each wave has a high point, called a peak or crest, and a low point, called a trough. If you were standing on a platform in the ocean, holding your hand out horizontally, as each wave passed by, the crest of the wave would touch your hand. The number of times that happened—that is, how many crests went by in each second—is called *frequency.* Frequency is measured in units of reciprocal time—that is, 1/second.

Ordinary light, coming from an incandescent bulb or even from the sun, is jumbled up. Its light waves vary in frequency. In contrast, all the waves of laser light are identical in frequency, since they originate from identical atomic transitions. The word used to describe frequency coherence is *monochromaticity.*

Scientists have discovered there is an electromagnetic spectrum of varying kinds of energy. The oscillations and waves within this spectrum produce both electrical and magnetic effects. Most of these energies are invisible. We can measure these waves, characterizing them by frequency and wavelength. For convenience, we divide the electromagnetic spectrum into sections. These sections are classified by the ways in which these energies are generated and used. The electromagnetic waves that have the lowest frequencies are radio waves. Next are the microwaves. Above the microwaves (but still invisible to us) are the infrared frequencies. We can feel these frequencies as heat, even though we do not see them.

Visible light is an extremely narrow part of the electromagnetic spectrum. The colors we know range from red, starting at a wavelength of 760 nanometers, to violet, which ends at a wavelength of 360 nanometers. (A nanometer equals one-billionth of a meter.) Above visible light on the electromagnetic spectrum come ultraviolet light, X rays, and gamma rays.

The "white" light from an incandescent bulb or the sunlight that we "see" is really made up of many different colors. You can prove this yourself by looking at a beam of light before and after it is passed through a prism. The prism breaks the light up into its different colors.

Laser light contains light of virtually only one color. This color can vary, of course. In fact, lasers can produce frequencies and wavelengths that range from those of infrared rays through visible light and into ultraviolet light. The light from any one laser is concentrated into an extremely narrow band of frequencies.

Direction and phase are also important concepts. Imagine a group of people who do not know each other walking across a bridge. They are not all moving in step. Some go one way, while others go another. Some people are a little ahead; others lag behind. Ordinary light has wave patterns like this group of people. It is called *spatially incoherent*. The waves do not come at regular intervals. They are not all moving in the same direction.

Laser light is different. Laser light has spatial coherency. Waves of laser light are somewhat like a large, well-disciplined marching band crossing the bridge—each row exactly the same distance from the row in front and in back. Because the band members are in step, every one of those hundreds of people puts his or her foot down at the same time, generating far more force than the random walkers. Laser light works the same way. Because it is spatially coherent, the electric field reaches a maximum for all the little wavelengths at the same time, acting in unison. It is the coherence of laser light that gives it such power.

MAKING THE FIRST LASER

By 1960, when Maiman was a Hughes researcher, scientists, were used to working with coherent light from radiation: ordinary radio waves, the AM radio, the FM radio, VHF (where television is on the electromagnetic spectrum), UHF (the higher bands of television), and even microwaves. If coherent light could actually be generated—and some leading scientists of the time believed this would never be possible—it would be an important step and a breakthrough, since light waves are about ten thousand times higher in frequency than the microwave section of the spectrum.

Maiman was eager to try.

He considered using potassium vapor, an idea Townes and Schawlow had suggested. He considered using an electrical discharge similar to that in a neon sign—an idea that other researchers had proposed. However, what he really wanted, he decided, was a simple, rugged, solid material—one that was fluorescent, so its crystals would glow under ultraviolet light. Since he was already familiar with the optical properties of the synthetic ruby crystal from his earlier work with masers, Maiman chose the ruby for his experiments.

One problem with using the ruby, however, was that ruby light might not be efficient. A paper had been published by another scientist, suggesting that if you stimulated the ruby by shining ordinary (incoherent) ultraviolet, green, or blue light on it, the ruby would glow red. Nevertheless, according to the published paper, the efficiency of that fluorescence was extremely low. The paper predicted that only 1 percent of the energy would be released in the red glow; the remaining energy would be absorbed in the ruby by the green light.

Maiman's own research had already showed him that to get atoms in the ruby crystal excited enough to obtain coherent laser light, he would need an extremely intense light to get the process going. An efficiency of only 1 percent would make using the ruby crystal impractical.

Consequently, Maiman abandoned the ruby idea. "I had no reason to doubt the accuracy of the measurements in the other paper," he was to recall. "I looked at a number of other fluorescent solids that might be more suitable. None worked. Each had their own problems.

"I returned to the ruby, trying to understand why the fluorescent process was as inefficient as the paper reported. There were a number of reasons why this could happen, I thought, and I looked at all of them, measuring carefully. To my surprise, I discovered the supposed inefficiency did not exist! Instead of having only 1 percent of the green 'exciting' light converted to the red light of the fluorescing ruby, I found that around 70 percent could be converted. Ruby became a real possibility.

"Not everyone agreed with me. I listened to a paper at a conference I attended in which Schawlow, from Bell Labs, said his group had evaluated the ruby and had concluded it was impossible to make ruby work as a laser. I wasn't disturbed by his conclusion. He thought it was impossible. I thought it would be difficult. But I felt strongly that it could be done, even though I was competing with world-class scientists."

His supervisors at Hughes questioned the real value of Maiman's project. They suggested that he switch to work on research into computers, but reluctantly allowed Maiman to continue his work on the ruby laser project. Maiman kept going, though he felt the company's financial and psychological support were meager.

"I stuck my neck out a mile," he said, "but the concept of being the first person to generate coherent light was exciting! I kept fantasizing about being able to pull it off, being the first in this technical Olympics."

By all Maiman's mathematical calculations, his device should have worked. Step by step, he checked and rechecked his measurements.

His ruby crystal rod was a rod 3/8 inches in diameter and 3/4 inches long. The ends of the ruby cylinder were flat, parallel, and highly polished. He made the ends of the rod reflective by depositing a thin coating of silver on them. He then carved away a small hole in the coating to allow the laser light to escape.

The crystal needed an outside energy source of extremely high intensity to excite the electrons. Maiman researched the characteristics of all known laboratory high-intensity lamps. He considered then discarded the idea of using a mercury arc lamp, though his calculations showed it just might work. "If I put my design together and it didn't," Maiman recalled, "I never would have known for sure if I'd failed because I didn't excite the electrons enough, or whether I failed because you never could generate coherent light."

Finally he decided to look at electronic flash. "I went through every catalog of every manufacturer," Maiman said. "I found three lamps listed. They were different sizes but all had approximately the same intensity. To be on the safe side, I sent for samples of all three; but since it was the energy per unit area that counted, I chose the smallest one to try first.

"Usually a lamp like this is mounted in a glass envelope, and its base fits into a socket. I cut off the glass and took off the socket, so I had the bare spiral flashlamp. I mounted the ruby inside the spiral. Around the spiral, I put a very highly polished aluminum reflector. The total housing was just a little smaller than a man's fist."

Maiman theorized that when he turned on the flashlamp, the strobe would put out an extremely intense burst of energy. The ruby crystal, he thought, would absorb that light. The ions would fluoresce and give off red photons. If he could get enough intensity, the red photons would not only glow, but would be amplified.

He predicted that it would take a very short time for light to travel along the length of the crystal and that the amplified light would start to leak out through the small hole he had made in the silver coating. Maiman set up a measuring apparatus, so he'd be able to confirm he had in fact generated coherent light.

Finally, there were no more problems to check out.

This was a moment of triumph. "I turned it on, and it worked— the first time! When the laser started to 'go', at first the fluorescence was at the low excitation rate. But as we got the excitation higher and higher, the crystal began to act as an amplifier. Then the photons that happened to be going along the axis of the cylindrical rod hit the mirror at one end and were reflected exactly back on themselves to the other mirror!"

Patent Problems

Maiman's achievement in building the first actual working laser was significant, significant enough for him to be named to the National Inventors Hall of Fame. There are only about sixty members, despite the four million or so patents in existence. Yet even though Maiman had an actual working laser—the first ever built— it was hard to sell his supervisors at Hughes and other scientists on his success and what it might mean.

In fact, the first scientific publication he submitted his work to turned it down. Finally, the British journal *Nature* published Maiman's results. A few weeks before the article appeared, Hughes flew Maiman to New York for a press conference to announce the working laser.

"That was my first encounter with media," Maiman was to recall. "I described how I thought lasers could be used in medicine and biology, in industry for cutting and welding, and in communications because of the information capacity and enormous possible bandwidth. One reporter asked, 'Is it going to be a weapon?'

"I told him I thought as a practical application of lasers, a weapon is a far-fetched idea. The next day, major headlines in the Los Angeles *Herald* said I'd discovered a science fiction death ray!"

Hughes lost foreign rights to the laser patents because they didn't file quickly enough. "In 1967, after I'd left and formed my own company to manufacture lasers, I found they weren't processing the patent efficiently. By mistake, I received correspondence between Hughes and the Patent Office saying the patent would be rejected unless a new argument was submitted within thirty days."

The Patent Office traditionally takes an adversarial view. In this case, the office told Maiman that since the ruby laser was "obvious," he shouldn't be entitled to a patent for making one. The office cited previously published papers by other scientists that it said proved their point.

"That infuriated me!" Maiman said later.

"I contacted the Patent Office. I told them if they correctly read the references they themselves had quoted and followed the calculations the other scientists had presented, they'd see I was right. The other scientists had said the ruby would *not* work.

"I gave Hughes the chance to use my affidavit, or to relinquish their claim and let me file. Executives at Hughes were delighted to proceed, using my arguments, and the patent was issued within two weeks!"

Even though he'd clearly made the first working laser, it took several years for trade magazines to be convinced lasers actually had value. That taught him a lesson—a lesson that is worth passing on to others.

"If you, have any idea you want to pursue, if you've really studied it and thought about it, despite the negative consensus by experts, then go for it! I still remember a class one scientist was to give at a university in the summer of 1960, a class he canceled after my press conference on lasers. One of his announced topics was, 'Why a laser cannot work.' "

CHAPTER 3

LASERS IN HEALTH CARE

Lasers had just barely been invented when they began to be applied to medicine. As early as the first half of the 1960s, lasers were used to treat skin discoloration and to repair detached retinas. By the dawn of the twenty-first century, laser surgery has become a well-established course of treatment and is used for all matter of illnesses. Lasers are used by medical specialists for everything from eliminating snoring to treating such life-threatening illnesses as cancer. They are used very intensively in procedures involving the eye, helping to correct astigmatisms and other vision problems, and having laser surgery performed on one's eyes is no longer considered risky or even particularly unusual. In 1998, the Food and Drug Administration even granted clearance to the first at-home laser medical device for people with diabetes. This device, the Cell Robotics' Lasette, is a portable battery-operated Erbium:YAG laser that diabetic patients can use to draw blood for sampling their blood/glucose level, which many patients have to do once or twice a day. With the introduction of the home laser test, which hurts less and is far more accurate, this process has become vastly easier, especially when testing young children.

Because lasers now have been integrated into so many aspects of medicine, it is hard to say precisely how much money is spent each year on laser surgery and treatments. The medical laser equipment market, one good barometer of the growth of laser medicine, hit an all-time high in 1995, when sales reached the $1 billion mark. The field of cosmetic medicine alone, which is one of the fastest growing markets for laser procedures, witnessed tremendous growth in the 1990s. In 1994, revenues for cosmetic laser procedures—including removing wrinkles, birthmarks, hair, scars, and tattoos—came in at more than $1.4 billion, with just over one million procedures performed. By the year 2000, it is expected that there will be more than three million procedures a year, with revenue over $3.4 billion. Part of the reason for this growth is that the "baby boom" generation is getting older, and many of those seventy-two million "boomers" will seek cosmetic cures for the regular symptoms of aging.

Scientific research into the possibilities of lasers in medicine also has been undergoing a boom. At large research institutes such as the Laser Center at Massachusetts General Hospital, medical researchers are working in a wide array of specialties, including cardiology, gynecology, neurosurgery, orthopedics, otolaryngology, and urology. Researchers at Emory University's eye center are using diode lasers to destroy the abnormal tissue in babies' eyes that leads to blindness, with a success rate of 90 percent. And at Loyola University Oral Health Center, oral surgeons use a device that looks like a ballpoint pen to perform biopsies and remove abnormalities from the mouth. These kinds of procedures sound like science fiction, medical practices from the distant future, but they are simply a sign of how advanced the use of lasers in modern medicine has become. In fact, says the American Society for Laser Medicine and Surgery (ASLMS), in some medical specialties, "virtually no practitioner works without a laser at hand."

The high intensity of laser light and the fact that it can be precisely focused allow physicians to control the cutting or cauterizing of living tissues. "You can make a precise cut with very little damage to surrounding tissue," explains Dr. Ellet Drake, the executive director of the ASLMS. One clear advantage of lasers is that they can be used without coming into contact with the region of the body being treated, so that there is almost no risk of infection. Because the laser coagulates (seals off) blood vessels that it cuts, the surgical site is almost bloodless, giving the doctor a clear view.

Laser surgery has traditionally worked best on soft tissue rather than on bone. Because thermal lasers work primarily through heating and cauterizing tissue, the intensely focused laser beam can burn a minuscule hole with great accuracy. In some cases, a series of these tiny holes are burned into the area surrounding a lesion, helping to seal it off. This procedure is somewhat like spot welding in a factory.

LASERS USED IN MEDICINE

In health care, three kinds of lasers are mainly used: the argon laser, the CO_2 laser, and the neodymium-doped yttrium aluminum garnet (Nd:YAG). The laser used for a particular medical procedure depends primarily on where the wavelength of that laser is best absorbed. For instance, the argon laser is effectively absorbed by tissues containing high concentrations of hemoglobin or melanin. Consequently, the argon laser may be the laser of choice for working with tissue where many blood vessels are involved, such as the retina of the eye or a portwine birthmark.

The carbon dioxide (CO_2) laser has a longer wavelength, one that doesn't really differentiate pigmentation. James Johnson, consultant in safety and laser applications and author of two books on lasers, points out that "any tissue that contains water will absorb the CO_2's wavelength. Thus, the carbon dioxide laser is extremely useful for surgery. It can vaporize tissue."

Although the CO_2 laser is used to cut out certain types of cancers, including cervical cancer, it has some limitations. Doctors using this laser have only "line-of-sight" vision. Light from the laser can be transmitted only through handheld lenses, through rigid scopes, or through a microscope. The beam of the carbon dioxide laser is transmitted only in a straight line or is reflected by mirrors. Scientists are working on allowing the carbon dioxide laser beam to pass through flexible fibers.

The Nd:YAG laser, on the other hand, can be used with fiber-optic technology. Optical fibers are extremely thin threads of glass that can transmit light over distance with very little loss of intensity. Rays of laser light traveling down such fibers are reflected off the sides.

In certain medical procedures, called endoscopies, the flexible fiber-optic device is used to let doctors look directly into portions of the body that otherwise they could not see, such as bile ducts or the lungs. Endoscopic examinations also allow doctors to treat certain conditions directly.

The Nd:YAG laser beam can pass through such a flexible scope and down to the area needing treatment. The surgeon can direct the laser beam to the target and use the beam to cut out tumors. "The YAG laser penetrates tissue very deeply," Johnson explains, "but its energy is dissipated because it scatters over a large volume of tissue; consequently it's good for cauterizing."

In photodynamic therapy a tunable—that is, an adjustable—dye laser is used. Here, doctors can aim the laser beam at tissue that has been treated with special chemicals. Laser surgery then selectively kills the cancer cells.

In one investigational procedure that used the argon dye laser technique, a special drug—dihematoporphyrin (DHE)—was injected into cancer patients with large tumors that interfered with eating and swallowing. The drug was taken up by only the cancer cells.

Light emitted by the tunable argon dye laser is sent down the long, thin, hollow tube, or endoscope, to the portion of the esophagus where the cancer cells are located. Because dihematoporphyrin (DHE) is a photoactive drug, it reacts when exposed to light of a particular color—in this case, the wavelength of the argon dye laser. The drug causes the cancer cells to disintegrate when the pulses of laser light hit them. Because the energy of electrons coming into the laser can be tuned, the resulting laser beam will be just the right wavelength to trigger the process and destroy the cancer cells by stimulating the desired chemical change.

Before this laser procedure was developed, these patients probably would have been treated with a different sort of laser in a procedure that can damage healthy unshielded cells in the esophagus as well as the cancer cells. The argon dye laser technique, therefore, is much more selective in the tissue damage it causes.

One doctor who investigated this technique was Dr. Stephen K. Heier at New York Medical College in Valhalla, New York. Heier found that the drug-and-laser treatment worked successfully to reopen the esophagus to near-normal or normal size. The patients found the procedure to be painless, and they were able to resume eating regular diets. Nearby normal tissue exposed to the laser light received only minimal damage from the procedure.

Extensive research is being conducted on other kinds of lasers for health care, including excimer lasers and free election lasers.

LASERS IN OPHTHALMOLOGY

In the early 1960s, soon after lasers had been invented, doctors and scientists began experiments to see if the technology could be used to treat eye disorders. By 1961 a group headed by Dr. Charles J. Campbell at Columbia Presbyterian Hospital in New York City became the first to use the laser to treat a detached retina. Several years later, Dr. Hugh Beckman used a laser to open tiny holes in the iris. This treatment, performed at Detroit's Sinai Hospital, demonstrated that lasers could be used successfully as a surgical instrument as well as in coagulation.

Today, this operation is routinely used to treat narrow-angle glaucoma. The tiny holes the laser makes in the iris let fluids flow easily again, thereby reducing the dangerous buildup of pressure caused when obstructions block the normal flow of fluid from the main body of the eye.

There are dozens of uses for lasers in eye surgery because lasers give ophthalmologists an enormous amount of precision and control. Lasers are most frequently used to treat retinal tears and detachments, diabetic retinopathy, and glaucoma. They are also used for resurfacing (plastic surgery), refractive surgery, and after-cataract surgery.

The argon ion laser, which uses a medium of electrically charged argon gas for generating laser light, is used extensively in eye treatment for a special reason. The argon ion laser gives off a blue-green light, a color that's strongly absorbed by red objects, such as blood. Many eye procedures involve sealing off blood vessels, so this laser becomes a powerful tool in coagulation.

Diabetic retinopathy is an extremely common complication of diabetes in which abnormal blood vessels develop in the retina. With the argon ion laser, the ophthalmologist can release up to three thousand laser bursts that strike the retina in a predetermined pattern. These short bursts of light can slow or stop bleeding from the blood vessels.

Argon ion lasers also are used to treat macula degeneration—an eye condition that often develops when a person becomes old. The macula is the central portion of the retina. If it becomes diseased, fluids can leak out from behind it and hamper vision. Because the laser coagulates, it can help reduce the leaking.

Lasers also are used to treat another form of glaucoma in which pressure buildup cannot be traced to a specific abnormality. The ophthalmologist uses the laser to make a series of openings in the tissues that normally let fluid flow out from the front chamber of the eye.

Ophthalmologists use the argon ion laser a great deal. In addition, they also use a krypton laser, which is similar in design. It uses krypton, another gas, as the lasing medium. Ophthalmologists choose these lasers because of their photocoagulation abilities. Although the argon ion and krypton lasers use an extremely small amount of heat, that heat can be delivered very precisely to the area the beam hits.

In addition, ophthalmologists like Dr. George Sanborn, associate professor of ophthalmology at Southwestern Medical School, University of Texas Health Science Center, Dallas, use the Nd:YAG laser to treat certain types of glaucoma. They also use it to treat a condition in which patients who have had previous cataract surgery and who have had an artificial lens implanted, develop clouding in a normally clear membrane behind the lens.

"The YAG does not use heat," Sanborn explains. "It's a disruptive instrument. It vaporizes the tissues it hits." Rapid pulses of the Nd:YAG laser eliminate much of the clouded area of the membrane, yet they keep enough of it intact to hold the artificial lens implant in place.

Still another type of laser, the excimer laser, is being tested for use in a controversial procedure called radial keratotomy. Some ophthalmologists are using radial keratotomy to make many tiny incisions in the cornea in an attempt to improve nearsightedness. Scientists who are studying excimer lasers think that perhaps the lasers can make fewer and shallower cuts in the cornea than the cuts needed when a surgical scalpel is used.

The carbon dioxide (CO_2) laser used in general surgery won't work for ophthalmology, Sanborn says, because vaporizing the tissue inside the eye would fill the eye with gas bubbles.

"Ophthalmologists today regard laser surgery as almost routine and not at all unusual," Sanborn says. "Today, most ophthalmologists receive training in laser surgery as part of their residency. Generally, they spend two months on the 'retina service' during their second year of residency, and that is where they're introduced to lasers in a structured program. By their third year of residency, they're using lasers (under supervision) to treat patients."

LASERS IN OBSTETRICS/GYNECOLOGY

Reproductive endocrinologists like Dr. Reena Jabamoni, a fertility specialist, are using lasers to help treat conditions that may interfere with conception. "The primary laser I've used is the CO_2 laser," she explains. "I use it for pelvic endometriosis, for reconstruction of the Fallopian tubes that have previously been damaged by endometriosis or pelvic inflammatory disease, and for removal of fibroids, which are benign tumors of the uterus."

Another type of laser, the endoscopic Nd:YAG, can be used to treat excessive menstrual bleeding not caused by an underlying disease. "I use the Nd:YAG laser to destroy the lining of the womb—a procedure that helps many women to avoid having a hysterectomy," Jabamoni explains. "However, this procedure makes a woman infertile, so it is used only when a woman plans not to have children."

One of the reasons for using the CO_2 laser in gynecology is that abnormal tissue can be vaporized or cut out easily. Gynecologists use the laser to remove lesions of the cervix, vulva, and vagina. Since much of a woman's reproductive system is accessible from outside the body, they also can use the CO_2 laser to cut out a tiny cone-shaped section of the cervix for diagnosis. Such "laser conization" can be done quickly and with virtually no bleeding. Women who do want to have children have very little risk of losing their fertility when this procedure is used.

Lasers also are used by gynecologists to treat other conditions. Genital warts, caused by a virus, can be removed with the laser—and the rate at which the warts seem to reoccur is substantially less than it would be with other forms of treatment. A laser inserted through a small incision in the abdomen can be used to treat adhesions of the ovary—a condition that affects fertility and occurs when the outside of the colon or another structure in the pelvis becomes attached to the surface of the ovary.

Reconstructive, surgery of the uterus is another area in which gynecologists can use lasers. "In a rare condition when a woman has a uterus divided into two compartments, I use the laser to take out the tissue between the compartments. Then the uterus becomes one full-size cavity that can hold a baby," says Jabamoni.

Procedures like laser laparoscopy are performed as outpatient ambulatory surgery, she says, while she has patients stay in the hospital when she is performing more extensive reconstructive laser surgery.

While many medical schools now routinely instruct residents in surgery and other specialties in the use of lasers, other doctors acquire these skills after they have already begun to practice medicine. Jabamoni began practicing in 1979, before lasers had fully entered the treatment of gynecological conditions.

"First, you take classes," she says. "Then you have hands-on experience in a laboratory, first in inanimate objects, and then with animal experiments. Next, you work with a preceptor—someone who has very good training. After the preceptorship, you will probably do a number of cases in a hospital setting, under the supervision of an experienced laser surgeon." Although the laser is precise, she says, "when you aim the beam, you are destroying tissue, layer by layer. Because you are working close to important organs such as bladder, ureter, and bowel, in vital areas of the body, you must be extremely controlled in your technique."

Keeping up with new developments in laser use is "mandatory," Jabamoni believes. She herself belongs to the Gynecological Laser Society and the American Society of Laser Medicine and Surgery and attends meetings of both organizations regularly.

LASERS IN PODIATRY

Podiatrists are using lasers more and more in their practices. Just how much more, though, depends on the type of practice a podiatrist has. Fortuneé Massuda, D.P.M., a Chicago podiatrist, estimates that only 5 percent of her work involves laser surgery. "That's because I see a lot of patients with bunions and hammer toes," she explains. "I don't use lasers for bone surgery, because I don't want to risk burning the bone."

Laser surgery is useful, she says, for soft tissue conditions: warts, plugged sweat glands, ingrown nails, and corns that are not due to a bone deformity. According to Massuda, laser surgery for these problems is simple, quick, and relatively painless compared to conventional surgery. "Patients aren't frightened by laser surgery," she says. "They're excited about it. They think it is magic."

In 1984, when Massuda bought the CO_2 laser she uses in her office, the price was $35,000. By 1999, these machines had become far smaller in size, and the price for certain lasers had dropped below $20,000, although some of the more advanced models became even more expensive.

From the patient's point of view, laser surgery is not difficult or prolonged. "My associate anesthetizes the area," Massuda says. "I go in, use the laser to cut out the diseased tissue and coagulate blood vessels. I complete the surgery quickly. For instance, I can remove one wart in two to three minutes—or a group of warts in less than ten minutes. My associate dresses the wound, and the patient leaves the office."

One important precaution: safety glasses. Massuda, the patient, and anyone else in the room wear them during the surgery because of the intensity and penetration power of the laser beam.

Like Jabamoni, Massuda was already practicing at the time laser surgery for podiatry became common. She received her initial laser training in seminars run by the company that sold her the laser. "That's the usual way," she says. "The vendor wants to be sure you are using the laser properly. You also want to be sure you have proper certification showing you know how to use lasers, in case you're ever sued for malpractice."

Laser companies often donate lasers to podiatry schools, so students can be trained in laser surgery. "It's good business for the companies," she says. "In addition to goodwill, they know that students who have done this surgery as part of their pediatric training will be comfortable when they use the laser. When they go into practice, they'll want access to a laser—either in their own offices, or in a hospital or freestanding surgicenter."

WORKING WITH LASERS

Although many doctors use lasers routinely in their practice, not everyone who works with lasers in health care is a physician. Laser nurses play an important role in hospital or clinic care. Sometimes these nurses also are designated as laser safety officers; at other times, the laser safety officer serves only in that post and does not function as a nurse.

A LASER NURSE COORDINATOR

At Wenske Laser Center, Ravenswood Hospital, Chicago, Robert Pyrcz serves as laser nurse coordinator and as laser safety officer. A graduate of Northeastern Illinois University in secondary education and U.S. history, Pyrcz spent ten years teaching mathematics to eighth graders in Chicago public schools before deciding to make a career switch. Although he enjoyed teaching, he didn't like being transferred to a new school every few years.

He wanted to work with people but found himself spending more and more time on paperwork.

Checking want ads to see where jobs were available, Robert found only one or two columns of classified ads for teaching positions—but four or five pages worth for nurses. Other family members who were nurses liked their careers and talked about them often; Robert thought he, too, would enjoy nursing.

He enrolled in Ravenswood Hospital's School of Nursing in 1981 and graduated in 1983. Because he'd had a number of science courses in his undergraduate studies, he could shorten the study time usually required for the nursing curriculum. He passed the state examinations and became licensed as a registered nurse (R.N.).

After working for a year in the rehabilitation unit, Robert saw an opening posted for a laser nurse. He interviewed with the hospital's medical director and was offered the position. Initially the hospital sent him to an intensive three-day workshop in Columbus, Ohio; after that, Robert says, it was basically "on-the-job" training, learning as much as he could from the physicians and by being around lasers.

Ravenswood Hospital (a major Midwest laser center) uses lasers in research, dermatology, general surgery, gastroenterology, as well as eye procedures and other medical specialties.

Pyrcz divides his time between the laser center and the regular operating room of the hospital. Patients who can have laser treatment using a local anesthetic or no anesthetic at all (such as eye cases or cases involving the removal of warts from feet) are treated in the center. Patients whose surgery requires general anesthesia receive laser treatment in the operating room.

Robert also spends time educating patients on the laser procedure—what to expect and how the healing process will go. "Many times they're a little afraid of the laser," he says. "They want to be reassured that it won't drill holes into them. I explain that laser surgery is extremely precise and talk with them about how it will help their condition."

Pyrcz assists surgeons during the laser part of an operation. He conducts workshops for nursing personnel, physicians, and biomedical technicians—a responsibility that takes up at least 30 percent of his time. Another 20 percent, he estimates, goes into public relations, such as speaking to various community groups. Half his time is left for patient care (including surgery) and patient education.

A Typical Day

On a typical day, Pyrcz arrives at work at 6:30 A.M. His first task is to check the surgical schedule to see what types of operations are going to be performed with the lasers.

He describes a day on which he found there were six laser operations scheduled in this way: "The first one was hemorrhoid surgery, with the CO_2 laser. Then there were two eye cases back-to-back. One was eye surgery to correct a condition that occasionally occurs after cataract surgery. We planned to use the Nd:YAG laser. The second was a panretinal photocoagulation to get rid of abnormal blood vessels that grow in the retina as a complication of diabetes—a procedure in which we would use the argon laser. Finally, there were three cases in a row in which we were destroying bladder tumors with a high-powered Nd:YAG laser."

For safety and security (since some of the lasers cost more than $100,000), treatment rooms containing them are kept locked. Robert, who describes himself as "the keeper of the keys," unlocks the rooms to prepare them for the surgeries. Additionally, each laser is locked with a separate key, which Robert carries.

"I wheel the laser into position," he says. "I prepare the operating table by draping it, and open up the instrument trays."

"I plug the laser in on its special electrical circuit, since it takes an immense amount of power. I also wheel in the smoke evacuator and set it up, to take the vapor caused by the impact of the laser beam on tissue out of the air."

Robert also makes sure the medical records for each patient are set out on the table, ready for the doctor. Careful, detailed records are kept by the hospital's medical records department and are used for analysis and reference.

For each procedure, the physician lists the power settings, the type of laser used, the amount of time the patient received laser treatment, how the laser beam was delivered to the tissue, the safety precautions taken to protect the patient, the verification of the patient's consent to operate, the type of operation performed, and the diagnosis of the patient's condition. As laser nurse coordinator, Pyrcz checks and keeps a copy of all this information.

Later, records will be analyzed so the hospital can determine general trends in laser surgery: What kinds of power settings are doctors using? What seems to be the standard mode of operation in a particular type of laser procedure?

Robert is present at all laser surgeries, both in treatment rooms and in the hospital's operating room. In the latter he is scrubbed, gowned, masked, and gloved. After the patient has been put under general anesthesia, Robert prepares the laser for use in a sterile field. He puts sterile drapes (or cloths) over the arm of the laser. He drapes the smoke evacuator to keep it sterile.

The physician tells Robert what power setting he or she has chosen for the treatment and whether he or she wants the laser beam delivered in a continuous wave or as short pulses. Robert adjusts the laser accordingly, making sure it is set properly and functioning correctly.

During surgery, as laser safety officer, he also has the responsibility of checking that safety procedures are being followed. "Everyone—including the patient—must wear proper eye protection at all times," he says. "The patient's operative site must be covered with wet towels to protect the surrounding skin that isn't being treated. I make sure the doors to the operating room are shut, that warning signs are posted showing laser surgery is going on, and that no one comes in or goes out. I make sure there is always water available, if a fire should occur."

If anything in the room, or during the laser surgery, does not meet Pyrcz's standards or satisfaction, he has the authority to stop the treatment and turn off the laser.

Even though normal working hours for Pyrcz are 6:30 A.M. to 3:00 P.M. Mondays through Fridays, with weekends off, he is on call for emergencies and has to wear a beeper. "I get beeped all the time when I'm in the hospital," he says. "Usually I can deal with the problem by phone. About four times a year I get calls at home. Sometimes I can handle the situation over the phone, but I'll generally get dressed and go down."

The salary for his position, says Pyrcz, is approximately $35,000 to $40,000. The three staff members he supervises (all of whom he trained) perform similar duties and receive approximately $28,000.

For a position like his, he says, a man or woman first must qualify as a registered nurse. "Then, if you have the interest, there are many workshops and seminars available so you can get the necessary training and continuing education hours you need to meet standards in your hospital."

A LASER COORDINATOR

At Rose Medical Center in Denver, Susan Hicks works in a job that is similar to Bob Pyrcz's. Susan studied sociology at the University of South Dakota, from which she graduated with a bachelor's degree in 1976. She also took courses sufficient to earn an associate degree in nursing. For a time she worked as a registered nurse (R.N.) in South Dakota.

A move to Denver gave her nursing experience in liver transplants and intensive care. She didn't enjoy rotating between day and night shifts, however, and, looking for stable hours, she moved to Rose Medical Center. After three years in the recovery room, she helped set up the center's first outpatient surgical area.

"The center bought its first laser in 1983," Susan remembers. "Since I was the most interested, I volunteered to take courses and learn more about it. I wanted to get credentialed in laser safety and help train other nurses."

Administratively, Susan's present position as laser coordinator combines many responsibilities of a laser safety officer with those of a clinical coordinator. She helps educate nurses on laser procedures. In addition, she is at the center for every laser surgery performed, making sure the equipment is properly set up and all safety features are in place.

Rose Medical Center has a number of lasers used for medical procedures, including an Nd:YAG laser and an argon laser for ophthalmology procedures, an argon laser for gynecological and dermatology surgery, two CO_2 lasers for general surgery, and a continuous wave YAG laser with fiber-optic capabilities that's used for pulmonary, gynecological, and gastroenterological treatment.

As she prepares operating rooms for surgery and checks laser safety features, much of Susan's work is similar to that of Bob Pyrcz's. She also is deeply involved in a center task force that is investigating how to start a laser program for vascular procedures. "I spend a lot of time with vendors," she says, "because as soon as anyone hears you have a laser program, they want to sell you something. I spend much of my time doing physician marketing, explaining the lasers and helping them (physicians) arrange a trial run, setting up a practice session for them with the equipment. I troubleshoot when there are laser problems or problems with related equipment, working closely with Bill Van Dyken, our biomedical technician. The laser is a temperamental machine, and it's good to have a backup person in the hospital. If I have to take the laser apart, forget it! Bill has a background of a medical engineer, and he can do it."

Since she comes to work at 7:30 A.M. and often doesn't leave until 6:30 or 7:00 P.M., it's a long day for Susan. Rose Medical Center has just hired an assistant for her, which will ease the pressure.

Getting out from under some of the responsibility will free Susan to complete other projects like the one she's started on eye testing for staff personnel. Certain wavelengths, like that of the argon laser, can penetrate right through the eye to the retina and can damage patients' or staff members' eyes if a stray beam escapes or reflects. Susan is making sure all staff who work with the lasers have received eye tests. Results are recorded in their personnel files. If they leave the center, their eyes will be tested again and records compared to be sure they haven't sustained any eye damage.

"Every day, I'm still finding out what my job is," Susan says. "It's a lot of hard work—but it's really rewarding."

LASER SAFETY OFFICERS

Not all hospitals have full-time laser safety operators. At Grant Hospital in Chicago, Frank Hurley, trained as a clinical perfusionist, carries the title of laser safety officer. But, says hospital administrator Jay Tuke, Frank may spend only one-third of his time on laser issues.

"Once things have been set up and are running smoothly," Tuke says, "Frank's time as a laser safety officer isn't that much. He does have to know how to operate the equipment, but for much of his day, he works as a clinical perfusionist."

Grant Hospital began offering laser surgery in the fall of 1987. A multidisciplinary laser committee considers and writes policies and procedures that Frank has the responsibility of enforcing. Sitting on the commitee are Frank, Tuke, a representative from obstetrics/ gynecology and one from gastroenterology, a biomedical engineering representative, and an administrator to whom operating room personnel report. The chairman of the interdisciplinary laser committee is the chairman of the department of surgery.

Grant Hospital uses its Nd:YAG laser for general surgery, such as mastectomies, thyroidectomies, hemorrhoidectomies, and some gastroenterological procedures. The hospital's CO_2 lasers are primarily used for gynecologic procedures, often for surgery related to infertility.

LASER EDUCATORS

Although many hospitals and medical centers offer laser courses to their own staff members, others bring in outside consultants to perform that function. Colorado-based Education Design is a company that puts on such courses for national and international clients. These courses can range from a three-page self-learning booklet on a technique, product, or procedure to a one-day workshop, to a textbook or training manual, or to a full five-day convention.

Another provider of laser education is Leadership Concepts Incorporated, in Wisconsin. This company deals specifically with lasers in health care and operating room management. "We help hospitals look at their program," says Carol Wirth, a laser educator and the president of Leadership Concepts. "If they don't have a laser program, we will do feasibility studies. We made recommendations for what type of program they should be formulating. We give them a program description; write policies, procedures, and job descriptions; and help them implement the program." Leadership Concepts Incorporated presents hands-on, two-day workshops that help nursing staff members at the facilities understand lasers and laser technology.

In addition, the company acts as an all-round resource for clients on an ongoing basis, keeping them aware of changes in technology.

A graduate of a nursing school in Janesville, Wisconsin, Carol worked her way up from a staff nurse at Mercy Hospital to operating room supervisor. Recruited by a Rockford, Illinois, hospital, she spent five years there, helping to develop programs to train staff personnel. At Rockford she saw firsthand the importance of laser training when the hospital purchased its Nd:YAG and CO_2 lasers. She had worked well with independent consultant Carolyn McIntee, who headed Laser Consultants, Inc., and the two joined forces in 1984 to form the new company.

Hospitals are eager for training courses in laser operation and laser safety—not only because they want to reduce their liability by being able to prove staff members have been properly instructed, but also because interest is growing. The prime benefit hospitals receive from these courses is having trained and educated personnel to run these sophisticated, yet hazardous, pieces of equipment.

Is a health care career working with lasers for you? Yes, say practitioners, if you like the medical environment, are willing to work hard, and are interested in keeping up with technological developments. Medical research is moving so quickly that continuing your education is a must in this demanding profession.

CHAPTER 4

LASERS IN MANUFACTURING

From the CD player and bar code scanner that we encounter each day, to the laser beams used by NASA to measure distance in space, lasers have found their way into every corner of our lives. Yet not only do lasers operate *within* these countless gadgets and high-tech miracles, they are often used to actually *build* the products themselves.

Lasers have certain advantages over traditional manufacturing processes. The special properties of laser light (monochromaticity, coherence, divergence, and brightness) make it particularly useful for many industrial practices such as drilling, cutting, marking, welding, heat treating, and cladding (a technique used to melt alloys and selectively deposit them onto surfaces of parts). Lasers also are used to strip wires, drill tiny holes for watch jewels, and even cut the cloth for the mass production of clothing.

Perhaps when you imagine having a career with lasers in manufacturing, you picture yourself standing at a table, aiming the laser at the item you want to cut or weld. In today's factories, however, the laser is rarely a "stand-alone" machine. It is usually part of an automated process, one that frequently involves computers and a number of steps.

A manufacturing system that uses lasers needs a way of delivering the part being handled to the workstation where the laser operation will take place and of taking the part away to the next stop after the laser process has been completed. The process also calls for a laser system capable of generating sufficient energy to perform the desired task, and a way of focusing the laser beam to deliver the energy to the "right" spot on the part (a task often handled by automated vision systems). Because only part of the electrical energy can be used as optical output (the laser beam), a laser manufacturing system needs a cooling system to get rid of the rest of the energy and resulting heat. If the laser process involves removing or vaporizing material (such as in drilling or cutting operations), an exhaust system is needed to remove smoke, gas, and particles of material from the workstation.

In addition, a manufacturing system involving lasers almost certainly will have a controller to make sure everything is happening for the "right" length of time and in the "right" sequence. It will probably also have an off-line programming system, so that changes in the computer program governing the operation can take place without having to shut the assembly process down. Although industrial lasers have been in use for more than thirty years, their popularity in the last ten years has surged, as more and more factories turn to high-tech processes. Initially, vendors supplied turnkey systems. Even today, the capital investment required for installing a large, powerful laser system is significant—often more than $500,000. However, technology has dropped the cost for certain kinds of lasers. Consequently, smaller factories are finding lasers affordable and are beginning to install one or two of them for "job shop" work.

THE ADVANTAGES OF LASERS

Lasers have several advantages over other manufacturing techniques. Although there is a high initial cost, and time must be dedicated to training workers to use lasers properly, they are still very economical.

For example, in traditional manufacturing processes such as welding, cutting, and drilling, tools come in contact with the parts being worked on. Friction and the abrasive contact between tool and part wear out machine tools, so they must be replaced often. Tool replacement is much less frequent with lasers, because the beam is performing machining operations without direct contact.

Since it is easy for the laser beam to be precisely focused, the energy needed to accomplish the work can be placed accurately. Very little of the material surrounding the site of the laser weld or laser cut is affected by the heat resulting from the energy that's delivered. Consequently, the material being worked on has less damage and waste. In traditional machining, sometimes as much as 90 percent of the original piece of metal is whittled away. Not so with lasers. Parts are less deformed. That's an important advantage when work is being performed on parts for an aircraft engine or when lasers are being used in small welded assembly jobs.

Another advantage of laser processing is its flexibility. It is possible to control the heat and energy of the laser by changing its settings to give the beam more or less power as desired.

One great feature is that engineers can quickly design specifications on their computers and transmit the instructions to the laser. This is far more efficient than waiting for the assembly line to be retooled. Now companies can alter the design of a product, make upgrades, and respond to changes in market demand quickly and affordably.

Speed is another important advantage that lasers have. In many cases lasers can process materials at a substantially faster rate than more traditional methods. The line, or job, moves faster—thus saving money.

Laser tooling also has the advantage of being very simple. Most lasers have multiaxis capability—that is, they can be positioned to work in different directions. If a part is round, or if laser work (such as a weld) must be done at a difficult angle, the laser tool can usually handle the job. Because the laser beam can be focused to a very small diameter, lasers can be used to work on areas of parts that otherwise would be hard to reach.

TYPES OF LASERS

Lasers used to process material are generally of two types: solid-state or gas. A solid-state laser uses a crystal for the lasing medium. A gas laser, such as the carbon dioxide laser (CO_2 laser) uses the gas as the lasing medium.

Some lasers, such as the neodymium-doped yttrium aluminum garnet laser (Nd:YAG laser) and the CO_2 laser, can be operated to produce a continuous wave (CW). Others, such as the ruby laser and neodymium-doped-glass laser (Nd:glass laser) are set up to provide short pulses of laser light. The Nd:YAG and CO_2 lasers also can be operated as pulsed lasers, if such a mode is appropriate for the desired material handling process. The solid-state alexandrite laser is another such laser that can operate either in a pulsed mode or as a continuous wave.

The choice of a particular type of laser to use depends on a number of factors, including the power range needed to perform the desired task. For example, YAG lasers are exceptionally well suited for precision drilling and cutting operations on a wide variety of inorganic materials where power ranges of 0.5 kilowatts or less are required. YAG lasers have two important advantages over conventional tools in these applications. The laser beam doesn't get dull or change its size or shape as a result of wear. In addition, the way the laser beam performs is not substantially affected by how hard or how machinable the piece is that the laser is working on.

CO_2 lasers are the powerhouses of industry. They're able to operate at power levels up to 10 kilowatts—often making them the technology of choice for heavy-duty industrial applications like cutting, welding, and heat treating. The CO_2 laser is also well suited for processing organic materials.

For applications needing low power, the YAG laser is generally chosen; for high-power requirements, it's the CO_2. In between, there's a narrow range of power requirements where either the YAG or CO_2 can be used.

YAG laser systems have successfully drilled a wide variety of high-temperature alloy aircraft turbine components, automotive gear and bearing materials, and other precision parts. In addition, they are used for cutting complex shapes in products ranging from steel automobile doors to titanium aircraft components, and for welding a variety of industrial products.

Carbon dioxide laser applications include cutting and welding a variety of metals up to twenty five millimeters thick; cutting, drilling, and welding plastics and such other organic materials as leather, wood, and paper; cutting and drilling glass, quartz, ceramics, and similar materials; and heat treating and surface treating a variety of metals. If desired, a CO_2 laser can be attached to a robot manipulator and used for production welding, cutting, heat treating, and similar applications.

If a manufacturer needs flexibility, a YAG laser and CO_2 laser can be combined on the same laser processing system. Both the YAG laser and the CO_2 units can be permanently attached and can share the same deliverly system for the laser beam. Or both laser units can be configured and installed as stand-alone units, so that the YAG laser and CO_2 laser have individual delivery systems.

Vendors work closely with factory engineers and process planners to match laser characteristics to application requirements in order to achieve maximum efficiency in a highly cost-effective installation.

For instance, Raycon Corporation, a leading vendor of laser processing systems, reported a manufacturer of jet engines needed a laser machine tool that would work well with many different aerospace metals, different-shaped parts that were being processed, parts that varied in size, and different processing applications. There was little room for error in finished parts; the machining tolerances were demanding. In addition, the parts being worked on had to be placed and held in an extremely accurate position so the laser beam could be focused at just the "right" point.

Raycon worked closely with the manufacturer to develop a general-purpose laser processing system that was both versatile and precise—while still meeting the particular application requirements. Although similar systems can be installed for other manufacturers, they too can be modified, either with commercially available equipment or with custom-made hardware. For example, a CO_2 or Nd:YAG laser can be equipped with a special nozzle assembly, with output power that's matched to a particular job, or even with a completely different machine control system.

LEARNING MORE ABOUT LASERS IN MANUFACTURING

Locating additional sources about how lasers are used in manufacturing is easy. Many of the books listed in Appendix B have information on various laser applications.

Current technical articles about "Lasers in Manufacturing" are listed in the *Applied Science and Technology Index,* which can be found on reference shelves in almost every public library.

An excellent source for papers on lasers in manufacturing is the Publications Division of the Society of Manufacturing Engineers, One SME Drive, P.O. Box 930, Dearborn, MI 48121-0930. The society's telephone number is (313) 271-1500. You can call or write for the current catalog, which lists the books, videos, CD-Roms, training programs, and technical journals published by SME.

Another rich source of information is SME's web site at www.sme.org. By searching the publications list you will find more than two hundred papers that contain information on lasers. Such papers as "Laser Selection for Drilling" and "Laser Selection for Cutting" give specific information about particular laser application. "Lasers in the Future" discusses growth trends for lasers that extend the capabilities of flexible machining centers, as well as for heat treatment by laser.

Reading papers like these will help you learn more about lasers in manufacturing and will give you a chance to see if a possible career in that field appeals to you.

Meetings and Conferences

Another way to learn more about lasers in manufacturing is to attend meetings at which they are discussed. On the local level, chapters of SME's various associations—especially the Computer and Automated Systems (CASA), the Robotics International (RI), and the North American Manufacturing Research Institution (NAMRI) divisions—hold dinner meetings at which speakers present various topics. Such meetings are usually publicized, and nonmembers can attend by registering in advance and paying a small fee.

Trade shows, such as SPOT (sponsored by SME) and DE-LASE (sponsored by SPIE—the International Society for Optical Engineering), are excellent sources of information. Smaller clinics, such as "Lasers in Electronics Manufacturing" (SME-sponsored), are focused on particular topics. Papers presented at these clinics often provide case studies of laser systems at individual firms ("Microelectronic Laser Welding—Proven on the Production

Floor") or offer discussions of technical and economic aspects of laser work ("Process in Laser Marking and Engraving").

Films and Videos

Another way of learning about lasers in manufacturing is to look at videotapes. SME's *Lasers in Manufacturing—A New Look* is a twenty-six-minute tape about fundamental operating principles, common benefits, and typical laser equipment available. Four case studies demonstrate how using lasers can improve manufacturing productivity and profitability.

At Defiance Metal Products, you'll learn how lasers are used in machining chassis parts. Next you'll see how a twelve-hundred watt carbon dioxide laser is used in the machining of Kevlar panels for jet engine nacelles at Laser Fare Limited. Quantum Laser Corporation uses laser technology in the cladding of machine tool components with hard, wear-resistant alloys. Finally, you'll see how low-powered helium-neon lasers are used for measurement at Laser Line, Inc.

SME also has videotapes that can be rented or borrowed by schools. A three-videotape program, "Adventures in Manufacturing," is available free of charge to schools, career counselors, and libraries. Well over a million viewers in school and community audiences have seen the career film, *The Challenge of Manufacturing,* which encourages young people to relate their personal interests and talents to a manufacturing career. The twenty-four-minute tape does not specifically target working with lasers as a career; however, it does show the factory environment, and it does discuss activities young people can do while they are still in high school to help prepare them for manufacturing engineering.

The other two videos in the "Adventures in Manufacturing" series are *Race Against Time* and *Engineering: Making It Work. Race Against Time* is aimed at college-level students and adult audiences. It focuses on trends and new opportunities in manufacturing, competition, automation and the computer, the teamwork concept, and the rewards of manufacturing. Examples from IBM, Briggs & Stratton, Intel, McDonnell Douglas, Ingersoll Milling Machine, and Seafreeze are shown. Also featured is commentary from prominent experts, including Dr. Tom Peters, author and consultant for business excellence.

Engineering: Making It Work is a short (thirteen-minute) video introduction to the ways that manufacturing influences every aspect of our lives.

Contact the SME Education Department for purchase or free-loan information. SME also has an educational web site for students and teachers. The Internet address is www.manufacturingiscool.com.

KINDS OF JOBS

There are several levels of jobs available for people who want to work with lasers in manufacturing, says Fred Seaman, laser veteran who heads F.D. Seaman and Associates and who spent more than ten years running the laser center at the Illinois Institute of Technology. There's certainly a need for people who are "doers" and who have only a limited knowledge about lasers. Often men and women who actually operate lasers in manufacturing come from other backgrounds. Perhaps they have been numerical control (NC) operators with previous experience in running controllers that oversee automated operations. With previous experience in machining or in tool and die work, Seaman says, they can begin to operate lasers after relatively minimal training.

Training for these people is relatively simple, Seaman thinks, and can be carried out by complex interactive graphics. At Ford Motor Company, Seaman says, a worker receiving such training watches a computer screen on which questions appear. If the worker gives the "right" answer, he or she continues on to the next question; if not, the screen displays an animated character who indicates the mistake.

Salaries at this level average approximately $12 per hour in direct take-home pay, $10 or $12 per hour in a job shop, and up to $15 an hour in the automotive industry.

The next level up from operations is maintenance, Seaman points out. Here, he believes, a worker needs at least a two-year educational program about laser principles. "He or she has to know enough about lasers not to get hurt, as well as enough to understand the purpose of what's being done with the laser," Seaman says. The maintenance worker will clean portions of the laser system periodically and replace worn parts. Usually the duties are limited to following a checklist, doing the items as predetermined. For example, one task might be "take out the lens and clean it." Another might be "check filter."

"After he takes a lens out, he has to understand what test he will use to see if he replaced it correctly," Seaman explains. "He or she may have to do some things with cooling systems, so the person must know a little about refrigeration. Most of the knowledge needed is taught at the two-year college level, in technicians' programs."

Maintenance people may receive $19 to $24 per hour and are likely to belong to a union.

Service personnel—a higher level than maintenance people—are generally employed by vendors and visit customer sites to fix problems or troubleshoot the laser system.

"They're detectives," Seaman says. "Although they listen to what operators and maintenance people tell them about what has happened and why the laser doesn't seem to work properly, a service person has to decide whether those people are really good observers or are merely passing on their preconceived ideas. Service persons need to work well under pressure and time deadlines.

They're under the gun from plant management. And sometimes they have to stand before the company's board of directors, explaining just why the expensive laser system isn't working."

Seaman says service people need a real ability to solve mysteries. In addition, they make their own observations of manufacturing processes, seeing what problems are happening and trying to clear them up. In order to identify problems, causes, and remedies, service personnel must know how to use typical electronic diagnostic tools, such as meters and scopes, and analytical optical equipment.

Salaries for service personnel run about $25,000 to $40,000 per year. Extensive travel may be involved, because service is performed at the client's plant, wherever it is located.

Above service personnel in this informal hierarchy, Seaman explains, are applications engineers. Often these are service personnel who have been promoted. They're employed by the laser manufacturer (the vendor of laser equipment) to work with potential clients before the sale is made—defining the client's actual needs and working out the fit with the laser manufacturer's products. Needed, Seaman says, is a combination of technical knowledge and sales orientation, along with extremely good listening skills and the ability to make presentations.

Generally these people hold a four-year degree, possibly from a technical college, in electronics, mechanical design, or a similar discipline. Speaking and writing abilities are vital, Seaman says, because the applications engineer must be able to hold his or her own in management arguments and must, in fact, help to convince the client company that the vendor's product is the right one to buy. Even though the applications engineer is not always officially part of the vendor's sales team, he or she plays an important role in making the sale. Applications engineers must be able to identify the customer's problems and come up with workable solutions that need the vendor's products to make them feasible.

Salaries for applications engineers are in the $30,000 range for those just beginning their career at this level. Experienced applications engineers can receive more than $45,000 in salary. In general, they are not on commission.

Slightly higher than the salary level of an applications engineer, but probably working in a corporate research laboratory rather than for a vendor of laser equipment, is a laser scientist. Laser scientists have a laser background. A typical job here might involve "marrying" a laser to a robot. While the applications engineer employed by the laser vendor might in certain circumstances receive more than $40,000 a year, laser scientists frequently earn well over $50,000. A few laser scientists become part of organizations that evaluate acquisitions—working for people who buy and sell laser companies.

The salesperson, or field representative, is probably a design engineer. Employed by the laser equipment vendor, he or she almost certainly holds an engineering degree from a four-year school. Added to that is a strong business orientation, including knowledge of business law, marketing techniques, and business administration. Although the salesperson does not have to have come up the ladder of experience as a service person and applications engineer, many do. Such a person has picked up the business law and marketing expertise—perhaps in night school courses—after the technical background and experience.

In one of the bigger laser companies, a salesperson or field representative could start at $40,000 and work up to $90,000 or more a year as district sales manager.

Holding a position comparable to that of the district sales manager (and earning approximately the same compensation) is a product design engineer, sometimes called an advance design engineer. Such a person has a university degree, Seaman says, and may have completed graduate work in engineering. He or she may work for a vendor, or such a person may be a scientist/entrepreneur who owns a small laser company.

JOB DESCRIPTIONS

The levels of involvement listed above may have different names in different companies. Whatever the job is called, you can be sure that somewhere there is a job description giving basic desired qualifications.

John Ruselowski, corporate sales director for Raycon Corporation, has provided four such sets of qualifications used by his company. By reading them, you'll have an idea of what persons holding those jobs actually are required to know and do.

Laser Product Technician: A person who could satisfy the required qualifications for this position would:

1. be able to read circuit diagrams and blueprints
2. have a general mechanical/electrical aptitude
3. have or be able to develop a knowledge of the primary process for which the machine was developed and be able to optimize that process
4. be working in the assembly area, preparing the machine for delivery and run-off

Laser Applications Technician: A person who could satisfy the required qualifications for this position would:

1. become very familiar with a machine's capabilities and be able to use those capabilities in a variety of applications
2. have a working knowledge of computer numerically controlled (CNC) equipment and machine tools
3. have a complete knowledge of CNC programming and be able to exercise the machine to its capability

4. have metrological and metalography knowledge for determination of laser sample dimensional and process quality
5. have a PC (personal computer) working knowledge for data organizing and result posting
6. be working in the applications lab

Laser Field Technician/Engineer: A person who could satisfy the requirements for this position would:

1. read circuit diagrams and blueprints
2. troubleshoot industrial electrical and electronic equipment on a module/board level
3. have a general mechanical/electrical aptitude
4. have a working knowledge of and be able to perform basic troubleshooting on a variety of machine CNCs
5. have a PC working knowledge for posting such items as repair requirements, hours, and parts replaced
6. be working in the field at the customer's site

Qualifications for each of the three jobs described above require a knowledge of laser safety. In addition, persons holding those jobs must have a knowledge of industrial lasers and be able to remove and clean optical components, align the laser optical resonator for peak output, adjust focusing optics, operate the laser controller, and change flashlamps or discharge tubes for both solid-state and gas lasers.

Laser/Electro-Optical Product Engineer: Under the supervision of the Product Manager-Lasers, this person is responsible for the engineering concerned with the YAG and CO_2 lasers and associated laser equipment that is incorporated in the company's machine tool product lines. This means involvement in the quotation stage to recommend a laser product that would satisfy the customer's needs, as well as recommending and overseeing mechanical and electrical design details that are associated with the incorporation of the laser into the machine tool product.

Other associated duties include documentation of design effort. The person holding this position must generate design specifications, test specifications, and test reports. In addition, the laser/electro-optical product engineer must generate quality control procedures, safety procedures, and service procedures.

Other duties in this position include assembling and generating mechanical and electrical drawings, a parts list, and user and maintenance manuals for the laser and associated laser equipment. Other people may help with the drawings and manuals if the machine tool's operation overlaps that of the laser.

To qualify as a laser/electro-optical product engineer, the person holding the job should have a bachelor of science degree in electrical engineering, with an emphasis on electro-optics. In addition, four years of experience with laser equipment is required. One year's experience should be with the integration of lasers and machine tools. This product engineer will have had laser training at various manufacturers' locations and, preferably, schooling in computer numerical control (CNC).

A LASER MACHINIST

In Phoenix, thirty-six-year-old Rick Jackson has had more than nine years' experience with lasers at Allied-Signal Aerospace, which is part of the Allied Signal Corporation. The story of how he was chosen for his position in the company's development department illustrates the idea of working your way up to running a laser.

As a Grove City, Ohio, teenager, Rick spent his last two high school years at Paul C. Hayes Technical School. After graduation, the school helped him get a job in a Columbus factory.

Rick was offered the option of three training programs. Gear grinding and boring mills paid more money. "But I was looking for the technology of the future," he remembers. "Numerical control (NC) machines were just starting up. I thought I could get in on the ground floor." Rick trained on NC drilling and boring machines and, he says, got a pretty good background.

But Rick was young and not ready to settle down. He left the factory and spent several years working his way around the country, taking whatever jobs he could find. By the time he was married and expecting his first child, he settled in Phoenix, hiring on at what was then Garrett Engine Turbines.

"After a year, I worked my way up from manual drills to NC machines," Rick says. "My technical school background and previous work experience helped me get the promotion."

"Three years later, I heard rumors we were going to put in a laser machining center. The idea of learning new technology had always been challenging and had served me well. Long before the laser actually arrived, I kept asking to be assigned to it. When it came in, I got the chance."

Today Rick works with a Nd:YAG pulsed laser that is used for cutting applications. In the company's research department, he says, workers are testing a high-powered CO_2 laser for heat-related processing.

Rick generally works six days a week, from 7:00 A.M. to 3:00 or 3:30 P.M. When he arrives, he first starts up the console; loading up the software sometimes takes long enough for Rick to go get a cup of coffee. By the time he returns, the machine's power supply has turned itself on and is warming up the circuits.

Next Rick references the laser. He needs to align the laser beam at the exact reference spot from which all cutting dimensions are determined.

A nozzle assembly on the machine holds the focusing optics that control the laser beam. That assembly rides up and down on a worm screw. The laser nozzle has no rotating parts.

In order to help position the machine, Rick has hooked up a TV camera that runs along the same path as the laser beam when it is machining. The TV screen is mounted right on the same assembly as the console. On the screen, Rick can see electronic crosshairs that help him place the beam in just the right spot.

To reference the machine, Rick positions it over a piece of scrap metal. He can place the machine precisely—within about 1/10,000th of an inch of where he wants it to be. Then he fires a single "shot" (or pulse of energy) with the laser to mark the metal part. The TV screen shows where the laser beam "hit." Rick needs to align the site hole to the electronic crosshairs on the TV screen. Once he has matched them precisely, he has a reference point.

All instructions to the machine as to just where the laser beam will cut are based on the distances from that reference point. These instructions have been worked out beforehand and programmed into NC tape. The tape goes through a tape reader, and the instructions are stored in the CNC microprocessor that runs the laser. Because the instructions can be retrieved and loaded into the computer's memory, Rick can modify the program if necessary, just as a secretary might edit a letter whose text has been stored in a word-processing program.

Usually the company's programming department writes the software programs that tell Rick's laser exactly where and how to cut the metal engine parts. That's because his machine uses two and three axes simultaneously as it makes the cuts in the metal engine parts. Rick, however, has enough computer knowledge to modify the program or to write one himself if the programming department is backed up.

Though much of Rick's computer-programming knowledge has been picked up on the job, he says he's learned a lot from a CNC programming course run by Arizona State University and taught to company machinists at their request. "Our company is very education-oriented," he says. "I'm taking college courses now to become more familiar with specialized materials and processing techniques."

Because Rick works in the company's development department, he handles a number of innovative designs from different divisions. "We prove out whether the work can be done," he says. "We get parts from not only one department, but from all over the plant." Since the company makes engine parts for airplanes such as Lear jets, Rick may test the practicality of laser cutting on everything from research combustors with thousands of holes; to sheet-metal casings for the engine, with perhaps thirty holes; to gears that need clearance holes drilled into them.

Though Rick's supervisor assigns priorities and plans Rick's approximate schedule, no two days are ever the same. Sometimes he spends 90 percent of his time running the laser, making the cuts as desired. Other days he encounters problems—and must take time to solve them, slowing down his output. Each metal Rick works with, from titanium to the exotic alloys used in aerospace manufacturing (Inconel, Hastelloy, Waspalloy, and Astrolloy), has its own characteristics, which may vary according to the grade of metal or alloy used. Rick must adjust his laser to achieve optimum cutting performance on each of them.

Though he could leave the laser running during his half-hour lunch break, he usually takes it out of cycle. Safety precautions he observes include shielding for the engine parts, since molten material is ejected from the laser cut. Rick wears laser safety glasses for the specific wavelength of his Nd:YAG pulsed laser. They have been ground to his prescription; a change, since until recently he had to wear laser safety goggles over his prescription lenses. The special glasses protect his eyes from any stray laser light or reflection. Like all company workers, he wears safety shoes on the job, a standard requirement in manufacturing.

The salary for a job like Rick's is anywhere from $30,000 to $40,000 a year—based on the length of service and a person's qualifications. Laser operators on a production line who just load parts and run machines are usually paid $12 or $13 an hour, but salaries can run to $60,000 a year for people who work in research facilities.

LIMITATIONS OF LASERS

At Whirlpool's Benton Harbor, Michigan, Research and Engineering Center, senior manufacturing research engineer Patrick Doolan works with advanced manufacturing engineering and advanced product development and research. Only one-fourth of his time is spent on lasers, he says. A former faculty instructor in welding at the University of Wisconsin-Madison, he was familiar with the ruby laser in the university's mechanical engineering department and suggested to Whirlpool that it could be used in process development work.

At Whirlpool's research and development facility, Doolan says, the Nd:YAG solid-state and CO_2 gas lasers are used. At the plants, low-powered helium-neon (He-Ne) lasers read bar codes and are part of scanning systems used to check the quality of prepainted steel. Whirlpool uses two CO_2 lasers at different plant locations for welding parts for making automatic washing machines. One laser welds a gear assembly. The other welds a stamped bracket to the tube that spins the wash machine's basket.

"No one has lasers only as their job," Doolan points out. "Once a laser system is in place in a plant, the laser becomes a part of several people's responsibilities. In one location, a process or manufacturing engineer might have it, with a person under him doing secondary machining operations with the laser. In another location, the welding engineer might take responsibility for a laser."

At the plant, the laser operator may check tools and specifically check parts, Doolan says, but the actual loading and unloading of parts to the laser workstation is automatic. The operator watches the overall machinery—one piece of which is the laser. Since the laser is simple to run, Doolan says, an operator can bring the system up quickly. Usually the laser requires little attention. Periodic maintenance involves cleaning and replacing the optical components, and for the CO_2 laser, changing the bottles of gas.

Doolan points out that lasers represent a major capital investment for a manufacturer. Depending on the complexity of the equipment, the cost may go as high as a quarter of a million dollars.

Generally, when lasers are chosen for a manufacturing application, they're put in to solve a special problem. "You really can't cost-effectively install a laser to replace a conventional operation that works well," Doolan says. "However, you may get a savings in cost of material. For instance, our gear assembly replaced a part made on a screw machine from a solid bar. We chose the CO_2 laser because it is the only way to make that particular gear assembly in two pieces and put it together. In our welding application, laser welding has a low heat input. Using the laser eliminated distortion and gave us quality improvement."

CHAPTER 5

LASERS IN MILITARY
AND SPACE APPLICATIONS

The military possibilities for laser were recognized soon after the technology had been invented. By 1965, the United States Army was developing a laser range finder. Because laser light can be used to measure distances extremely accurately, airplanes and tanks are often equipped with laser range finders. Usually, the Nd:YAG laser is used, sending out pulses of light to the target. When these pulses, which are invisible to the human eye, hit the target, they are reflected back to the sender. A computer carried by the airplane or tank can measure the time it took the pulses of light to make the round-trip and can then calculate the distance to the target. Smaller range finders have been developed that can be carried by individual soldiers working as forward observers. Soldiers equipped with individual range finders can provide distance readings to long-range artillery gunners.

THE STRATEGIC DEFENSE INITIATIVE (SDI)

One of the more well-known instances of the military development of laser technology was for the Strategic Defense Initiative (SDI). SDI was a U.S. military research program for developing an antiballistic missile (ABM) defense system that was first announced by President Ronald Reagan in a speech in 1983. The concept of SDI was a radical break with the nuclear strategy that had governed U.S. military policy since the development of the arms race. The system that Reagan proposed would provide a layered defense of the United States using futuristic weapons, some of which were only in the earliest stages of development. The idea behind SDI was that the proposed weapons, which included space- and ground-based nuclear X-ray lasers, subatomic particle beams, and automated space vehicles, would intercept incoming missiles high above the Earth. Supporting the weapons would have been a network of space-based sensors and specialized mirrors for directing the laser beams toward targets, and the entire operation was to be controlled by a supercomputer.

The plan also called for space-contained laser battle stations. Each battle station would consist of an assembly of laser devices put together in modules. Once these stations were placed into orbit, they could engage ballistic missiles launched from anywhere on the Earth, including those launched from submarines and intermediate-range ballistic missiles.

The direct energy weapons technology for SDI called for the space-based lasers to destroy or identify decoys while they are still in midcourse flight and to defend U.S. satellites. Since the beam of some types of space-based lasers can penetrate the atmosphere down to the tops of clouds, it was hoped that the space-based lasers would help defend the United States against missiles sent from aircraft and from tactical ballistic missiles.

Since 1970, Department of Defense researchers have been working on chemical lasers fueled with hydrogen fluoride for possible use as space-based lasers. Such lasers operate in the infrared section of the electromagnetic spectrum at wavelengths of 2.7 micrometers.

Other "candidates" for space-based lasers were devices that generate beams at short wavelengths of about a micrometer or less. Because brightness increases in a ratio of 1/wavelength square, being able to use shorter wavelengths can make the laser light much brighter if the quality of the optics and the accuracy in aiming the laser also are increased proportionally. Two of these lasers with shorter wavelengths are the radio-frequency-liner accelerator (linac) free electron laser and the short-wavelength chemical laser. In another approach, researchers have worked with nuclear reactors to pump a short-wavelength laser.

The Strategic Defense Initiative was nicknamed "Star Wars" after the popular 1977 science-fiction film. It was seen by its critics as unrealistic and even dangerous. In an April 1987 debate between General James Abrahamson, director of the Strategic Defense Initiative Organization, and noted astronomer Dr. Carl Sagan, director of the Laboratory for Planetary Studies at Cornell University, Sagan called SDI "an immensely dangerous and foolish scheme." According to Sagan, 70 to 90 percent of the members of the National Academy of Sciences in the relevant disciplines of mathematics, physics, and engineering said that SDI would not work. SDI was also extremely expensive. The original projections ranged from $100 billion to $1 trillion.

One of the rationales behind SDI, besides its protective function, was that scientists in the Soviet Union were working on lasers powerful enough to destroy low-orbiting American satellites and damage those further away. There was also concern that once SDI began to be implemented, the Soviet Union would develop its own lasers to threaten the U.S. satellites in the program. A report in 1985 by the U.S. Department of Defense and the Department of State said that the Soviet Union's laser program already employed more than ten thousand scientists and engineers conducting research in the three types of gas laser considered most promising for weapons applications: (1) the gas-dynamic laser, (2) the electric discharge laser, and (3) the chemical laser. The Soviets also were said to be working on short wavelength, excimer, free-electron, argon-ion, and X-ray lasers.

However, with the dissolution of the Soviet Union in the early 1990s, the signing of a series of arms control treaties, and the election of Bill Clinton as president in 1992, the budget for the Strategic Defense Initiative was cut back. In 1993, under the direction of Defense Secretary Les Aspin, the Ballistic Missile Defense Organization (BMDO) was established in place of the SDI. Instead of using costly space-based defense weapons, BMDO relied on ground-based antimissile systems. Following the curtailing of SDI, more emphasis was placed on the concept of ground-based lasers to track and hit missiles. While the budget for SDI had been literally astronomical, actual expenditures amounted to about $30 billion. In contrast, the initial annual budget for BMDO was $3.8 billion.

THE BALLISTIC MISSILE
DEFENSE ORGANIZATION (BMDO)

The Ballistic Missile Defense Organization is central to the effort to uncover the military potential of lasers, and work on lasers also is being conducted by other branches of the armed forces. By the late 1990s, the BMDO program had created most of the key elements necessary for deploying a space-based laser, or SBL, which would be one of the most advanced defense weapons ever designed. It includes a high-energy beam generator named Alpha. Since 1991, Alpha has performed megawatt-class lasing in numerous tests, and by 1999 it was performing at near-weapons class efficiency.

Another laser-related initiative was the Large Optics Demonstration Experiment initiated in 1987, and the four-meter-diameter Large Advanced Mirror Program (LAMP) in 1989. Since then, tests have been ongoing on improved mirrors and optics. The high-energy beam LAMP mirror is the largest mirror ever constructed for space use (the Hubble mirror measured 2.4 meters).

The goal of the BMDO is to integrate the high-power chemical laser components with other technologies being deployed in space. Thus, one experiment, entitled the Alpha Lamp Integration experiment, involved the megawatt class Alpha laser, the 4-meter LAMP primary mirror, and beam alignment and control technologies. At this point the coordinated experiments of this complete high-energy laser beam are being conducted on the ground.

As the threat of strategic nuclear war diminishes, BMDO research in free electron laser and neutral particle beam technologies has been discontinued. At the same time, the military has shifted to working collaboratively with civilian businesses for nonmilitary applications. The research originally developed for SDI and BMDO is spinning off into commercial applications, and some of the technologies have even found their way into medical care and entertainment-related products.

LASER DEFENSE AND WEAPONRY

Other laser-related military projects includes a laser satellite communications system, which is being considered for implementation by both the Air Force and the Airborne Reconnaissance Office. The Tactical High Energy Laser (THEL) is being developed by the U.S. Army Space and Missile Defense Command. This project will be the world's first laser-based air defense system. THEL is being developed in order to respond to "theater threats"—attacks by short-range rockets and artillery, cruise missiles, and pop-up helicopters that happen quickly and without much warning. The speed-of-light response of a laser is considered the only way to effectively react to such sudden attacks. In a 1996 flight test, a high energy laser was able to target and shoot down an operational short-range rocket. More field tests will be conducted in collaborative exercises with Israel, a country that needs a rapid-response defense system.

The presence of land mines has always been of great concern to the branches of the Armed Services that deploy ground troops. The Army, Navy, and Marine Corps have begun coordinated efforts to use advanced technology to detect these mines. For example, the Navy has successfully tested a laser line scan system for detecting mines in shallow water, and the Army is nearing completion on a vehicle-mounted mine detector and mine hunter-killer.

JOBS IN MILITARY PROGRAMS

Working with lasers as a member of the U.S. armed forces is another way in which men and women can find careers in laser technology. The first step in joining the armed forces is to talk with a recruiter. Your high school or career center counselor can put you in touch. Or you can check your local telephone book for listings. You can sign up at seventeen with parental consent; eighteen without it. More than 92 percent of young men and women being recruited have a high school diploma. In addition, you'll need a personal record good enough to stand a thorough background check.

You'll be given the Armed Force Qualifications Test, as well as the Armed Services Vocational Aptitude Battery. Your scores on those tests, as well as your interests, will determine what career paths are open to you. So will the particular needs of the service to which you are applying.

When you see a career counselor at the military entrance processing station, he or she will check your scores and show you a computer screen. "On the first screen you see will be the categories the service really needs to recruit people for—at the highest level for which you qualify," says Lt. Col. Greg Rixon, Army spokesman. "The computer is updated daily to reflect current needs."

If you are joining the Army, you might see a screen about Category 39E—a job classification with duties involving intermediate-level maintenance and repair on special electronic devices, such as mine detectors, battlefield illumination systems, warning systems, and various sensors. Although you will undoubtedly work with equipment other than lasers, laser technology will probably be involved in some of the sensing mechanisms. Training required for categories such as 63E (M1 tank systems mechanic), 45Z (armament and fire control maintenance supervisor), or 41B (topographic instrument repair specialist) also will probably include working with laser technology.

"We're giving recruits a contract we will honor," says Army spokesman Rixon. "For instance, if you sign up to be in Category 39E, you are going to be one—as long as you complete the training we offer for that category."

MEASUREMENTS IN SPACE

Using lasers to measure distances in space has helped scientists learn more about the universe. Complicated mathematical models of how the universe acts have been devised, and extremely precise laser measurements help calculate "real" ranges. By comparing the predicted distances with those that have actually been measured, the Earth's orientation can be monitored. Because the number of permanent lunar laser ranging stations around the globe is increasing, scientists can look for plate tectonic motions that will aid in predicting earthquakes. Data from these ranging stations are also helping to determine tidal effects and changes in the earth's rotation (shown by a change in the length of a day).

In the 1950s a group of physicists at Princeton University suggested using powerful, pulsed searchlights on the earth to illuminate mirrors placed on satellites in orbit. By photographing a satellite's position with respect to the fixed background of stars, they hoped to analyze the characteristics of the satellite's motion while in orbit.

Once lasers had been invented, however, the scientists' plans changed. Because laser light has a precise wavelength, and because laser light can be produced in incredibly short pulses, measurements in space can now be made with remarkable precision and accuracy.

LASERS ON THE MOON

In 1969, as part of their moon mission, Apollo 11 astronauts placed special reflectors on the moon's surface. Later, scientists from McDonald Observatory at the University of Texas at Austin aimed pulses of light from a ruby laser at these reflectors. The length of time it took the laser pulses to hit the reflectors and return was measured extremely carefully. Then scientists calculated the distance to the moon (238,857 miles between the center of the earth and the center of the moon.) Because the electronic circuits that measured the time were so sensitive, scientists believe the distance to the moon has been accurately measured to within two or three meters. New permanent lunar laser ranging stations have been added: at Grasse, France; at Mount Haleakala on Maui; at a site thirty miles south of Canberra, Australia; and at a site near Wettzell, in southeastern West Germany. Mobile lunar laser ranging systems are operating in the Netherlands and in West Germany.

JOBS WITH LASERS AND SPACE

Finding employment as a laser technician or scientist in the space program or related fields will most likely require an advanced degree. However, if working in this field interests you, you can contact university researchers, such as those at the University of Texas at Austin, or at other institutions studying these problems. You can certainly ask to be placed on the mailing list for bulletins, publications, and news releases about developments. And you may be able to use the information you get from reading the releases to contact some of the scientists mentioned directly. Sometimes, an individual scientist is willing to correspond with a young person, offering advice and suggestions.

CHAPTER 6

LASERS IN COMMUNICATIONS

One of the fastest growing applications of lasers is in the dynamic area of telecommunications technology. Until recently, telecommunications was primarily electronic. In the 1960s and 1970s, the development of silica glass fibers made it possible to use light waves to transmit large amounts of information over long distances. In the 1980s, optical fiber systems increased the capacity and speed of transmission. By the beginning of the twenty-first century, telecommunications has begun to rely on photons. Light, traveling as photons, or tiny packets of radiant energy, can move extremely quickly, allowing various forms of communications—text, sound, images, data—to be routinely transported over huge distances. This process uses semiconductor lasers, which transmit the light pulses carrying billions of bits per second of information over hair-thin glass fibers.

The use of photons to transmit information is part of the field of "photonics." Photonics, in its broadest definition, includes all the elements of optical communications. And the business of photonics is booming. Indeed, the amazing developments taking place at major research facilities are occurring so fast and furiously that groundbreaking discoveries are almost out of date before they have even fully entered the marketplace. The increased role of the Internet and a growing demand for optical technology in data storage, imaging, and switching means that this field will continue to expand in the future. Although the era of photonics only began in the 1980s, by 1997 photonics-related investments totaled over $2 billion. And whether you would like to work in a large research facility or at a smaller company, the opportunities for employment in this field are very promising, as there are now several thousand photonics- and optics-related companies in the United States, many of them operating in the field of communications.

BELL LABORATORIES

Originally part of AT&T, Bell Labs is now the research and development arm of Lucent Technologies, with locations throughout the United States and in more than twenty countries around the world. Altogether, there are over twenty-four thousand people working for Bell Labs in such areas as microelectronics and digital signal processing, software and information sciences, optical networking technologies, wireless and photonics, image and speech processing, distributed computing, and Internet and access technologies.

Bell Labs has played a critical role in the history of the laser. It was 1960 when Ali Javan and his coworkers at the Bell Telephone Laboratories first operated the helium-neon gas discharge laser, some months after Ted Maiman had created the first working laser at Hughes Research Laboratories. Bell Labs scientist Arthur Schawlow (who in 1981 was to share a Nobel prize for his work in laser spectroscopy) and his brother-in-law, Charles Townes (a Nobel winner in 1964 for his work with the ammonia maser), were awarded a significant patent in 1960—a patent that they subsequently licensed to laser manufacturers. By 1961, Bell Labs had developed the continuous-wave solid-state laser (neodymium-doped calcium tungstate). And a significant advance in light transmission of information came in 1970, when Bell Labs scientists developed a tiny solid-state laser capable of emitting usable amounts of concentrated light continuously at room temperature. By 1977, AT&T had installed the world's first light-wave system to carry voice, video, and data communications traffic in Chicago.

The developments in laser research continued apace at Bell Labs in the years before and after the Bell research community became a part of Lucent Technologies. In more recent years, researchers at Bell Labs (in collaboration with scientists at Yale University and the Max Planck Institute of Physics in Germany) have worked on novel semiconductor microlasers that use "bow ties" of laser light to emit highly directional beams with more than one thousand times the power of conventional, disk-shaped microlasers. These new microlasers are so small that hundreds could fit on the head of a pin.

Scientists at Bell Labs also discovered a way to make one laser do the work of 206 lasers. Using a single laser to generate light pulses (each lasting merely one hundred millionths of a billionth of a second), data were transmitted over 206 wavelengths, or colors, of light. (When data are transmitted, they are in the ones and zeros of digital information.) This transmission was the largest number of channels of communication every generated.

And in March 1999, at the one hundredth anniversary meeting of the American Physical Society, scientists from Bell Labs unveiled the world's highest power mid-infrared semiconductor laser. This new, experimental quantum-cascade (QC) laser has more than a thousand times the output of any commercial semiconductor currently operating in the mid-infrared wavelength region. Based on quantum physics and atomic layer control of semiconductor structures, the QC laser can be operated at room temperature, so it is more affordable than other semiconductor lasers. QC lasers operate like an electronic waterfall. The electrons cascade down an energy "staircase." Along the way, as they hit each "step," they produce photons (light pulses). Earlier QC lasers had twenty or thirty steps for the electrons to cascade down; in the newest version, electrons moved down seventy-five steps. The QC lasers, which were invented by scientists at Bell Labs, are being developed for commercial use in areas such as collision avoidance, pollution monitoring, and medicine.

OPTICAL NETWORKING

By the mid-1990s, the phenomenal growth in the areas of Internet access and high-speed data transfer would require Internet service providers (ISPs) to increase their fiber optic network capacity. Whereas only a few years earlier innovations like 56k modems had seemed fast to the average consumer, now users expected much faster connections. One option was to increase capacity by adding more fiber lines or by increasing terminal speeds with newer multiplexing systems. Yet by the end of the decade, it had already become clear that faster, more economical technologies needed to be developed in order to meet the additional demands. For that reason, Bell Labs and other research facilities are dedicating tremendous resources to developing optical networking systems, by which beams of light are used to transmit information directly through the air.

In 1995, technology developed at Bell Labs came together in the first optical-networking system to use dense wave division multiplexing (DWDM) technology. This technology is used to expand the capacity of fiber-optic networks. Three years later, Lucent Technologies rolled out an optical networking system developed by Bell Labs that is capable of delivering up to four-hundred gigabits (billion bits) per second of information over a single strand of fiber. This immense amount of information is roughly the equivalent of transporting the traffic of the entire Internet at any given second over one fiber.

Another breakthrough optical networking system developed at Bell Labs was Lucent's WaveStar™ OpticAir™ system. This system uses beams of light to transmit information directly through the air using lasers, amplifiers, and receivers that can be placed on rooftops or in office windows. The earliest applications of this wireless technology is expected to be in metropolitan areas and campus environments—places where geography or other constraints may make fiber connections harder to establish.

LASERS AND OPTICAL STORAGE

You may already know that lasers play an important role in compact disc technology. Since their introduction in 1983, the audio compact disc player and CDs have become "must haves" in every American home, car, and office. The compact disc has billions of microscopic pits on its aluminum surface. In these pits, music is stored in digital form. During playback, a laser beam scans the pits as the CD is spinning inside the player, sending the information from the pits to a computer chip, which converts it into sound.

Optical data storage, however, offers more advantages than merely high-fidelity music reproduction. An optical disc that's smaller than the familiar computer floppy can store the equivalent of a quarter of a million pages of typed information.

Originally, optical discs had ROM (read-only memory). Now, companies have developed erasable-disc technology. In May 1988 Tandy Corporation announced plans to license rights to the dye-polymer technology, which uses a high-intensity laser beam to encode a disc that's specially coated and a lower-power laser beam to read back the information. Hitachi and Sony also have worked on similar technology. R&D experts in other corporations have developed erasable disks for computers that are based on a technology that uses a laser for changing magnetic properties.

Even today's optical disc technology is speeding computer operations. Banks using optical discs from Bell & Howell find that information from multiple workstations is quickly accessible.

For instance, when a customer comes in to apply for a loan, the person taking the information can tap into the bank's mainframe database and use its information to help assess the creditworthiness of the applicant. Credit histories, credit checks, and other documents relating to that customer may be scattered throughout bank files. Optical disc storage and retrieval, however, lets the loan officer access the information randomly and quickly.

What does this technology mean to you?

If you want to work in this fast-paced, competitive environment, you must keep up with developments. Read magazines like *Time, Business Week, Fortune,* and *Forbes.* You also will enjoy reading the computer and Internet magazines. Check library indexes for the *Wall Street Journal.* Find the major companies researching this technology, write for annual reports, get on the company mailing list for press releases, and write to the appropriate personnel offices to learn of job openings and required qualifications. Many companies maintain elaborate web sites, such as Lucent's site at www.lucent.com. Because of intense competition among the companies, skills in sales and marketing will be important tools as you look for jobs—along with the ability to understand the technology and to help predict its advantages. As *Time* magazine reports, "The alluring glow of optics is pointed straight toward profit increased productivity."

HEWLETT-PACKARD LASERJET PRINTERS

The company Dave Packard and Bill Hewlett started in 1939 in a garage behind the Packards' home in Palo Alto, California—with $583 in capital—has grown to one of the top hundred industrial corporations in America, with net revenue of more than $47 billion in 1998, including computer-related revenue of $39.5 billion. Although HP makes more than ten thousand products, one of its best-known is its desktop laser printer. The LaserJet, LaserJet PLUS, and LaserJet Series II printers work with more than six hundred of the most popular software programs. Introduced in 1984, when the company "broke the barrier of the $100,000 laser printer" by inventing the desktop LaserJet for under $5,000, the printers have been a runaway best-seller. In fact, more people own LaserJet printers than all other laser printers combined. In the $13 billion computer printer market, Hewlett-Packard is clearly the leader, employing more than 124,000 people.

"A laser printer is based on copier technology," explains Jeri Peterson, press coordinator, Hewlett-Packard Boise Printer Operation. "There's an internal laser in the printer. When you type information into your PC via a software package, that data is transferred to the printer. It controls where the laser beam writes by exposing an area on a round photosensitive drum.

"As the laser beam moves across the drum, it exposes just a tiny dot on the drum. That laser has the capability of defining three hundred dots across and thirty dots down in each inch, giving it quality almost equal to that of a daisywheel printer.

"As the laser exposes the part of the photosensitive drum, it changes the electrical charge on the drum. The laser moves quickly while the drum rotates into another area within a toner cartridge. The toner, which has an opposite charge, is attracted to the area where the laser wrote on the drum.

"As the drum rotates, it passes over the paper, which is underneath the drum. Beneath the paper is a corona wire, carrying a charge opposite to that of the toner. Consequently, the toner is attracted to the paper. Next, it travels through a fusing unit (395°F) that melts the toner to the paper."

One big advantage of laser printers is that they're quiet, flexible, and fast. Because they're not tied to a font ball, like a daisywheel printer, users have the ability to integrate text and graphics—in effect, doing desktop publishing.

A PRESS RELATIONS COORDINATOR

Jeri Peterson didn't expect to be handling press relations for HP's Boise Printer Operation when she finished two years at a junior college in Yakima, Washington. In fact, she wasn't sure just what she wanted to do, so she tried several fields. She was a nanny for a California family, a hospital phlebotomist in a medical lab, an *au pair* in Paris where she worked for her room and board while taking French classes, and—eventually—a college student again when she realized she needed a degree. Earning her bachelor's degree in fine arts from the University of Washington, Seattle, she signed up for a campus recruitment interview. HP was looking for an industrial designer, but hired Jeri as a graphic designer in the disk memory division that makes large disk drives for HP's minicomputer systems. By 1984, when HP introduced the new Laser-Jet technology to dealers, a new system of marketing was needed; Jeri was on the ground floor. HP uses a "Dealer Channel" group as support for dealers. "I supported the Eastern region, doing dealer presentations," Jeri remembers. "I wrote proposals and documentation for desktop publishing applications."

By March 1987, when HP introduced the LaserJet Series II (a second-generation printer), the company essentially was making two earlier models obsolete. New sales promotion, effective for dealers, was needed if HP was to meet its goal of adding unit sales to make up for rolling over the higher-priced models. A time crunch came up, and Jeri found herself coordinating fourteen separate promotion projects.

Today, based in Boise, Idaho, Jeri deals mainly with the computer trade press. She's responsible for talking with editors when they phone, finding out what they need, and setting up interviews with on-site management people. Surveys show that PC-oriented consumer publications and trade press reviews play an important role in the user's buying decision, so the impact of successful public relations is strong.

Since HP has flexible hours, Jeri picks her own starting time, generally choosing to begin work at 6:00 A.M. If editors are visiting, she dresses more formally; otherwise a casual dress is fine, she says. One recent day found her awaiting an editor who wanted to write about HP's technical service phone line and who wanted to interview the college students who work part-time and take as many as twenty thousand phone calls a month from HP customers. Before the editor arrived, Jeri had briefed the service line's manager on kinds of questions the editor might ask and how to handle sensitive issues. After a ninety-minute meeting with the manager, she made sure all was ready for the continental breakfast she'd planned.

Jeri sat in on the interviews—not to censor them, because she generally doesn't even talk during them, but to make sure that the HP manager covered key issues. "If there's confusion, I'll restate the question," Jeri says. All went smoothly, but she also sat in as the editor spent an hour with a student who was manning the lines. By the time she returned to her desk, she found ten pink slips—phone calls from editors of other publications and from market analysts. "Although I'm not the HP spokesperson on strategic issues," Jeri says, "I do spend time talking with my managers, getting them to return calls. I brief them on who the editor is, so that when an article does appear, the HP message generally comes across."

Another component of Jeri's job is responsibility for product introduction public relations. HP currently uses a Los Angeles–based agency for writing news releases; Jeri coordinates with the agency, often traveling there to discuss sales promotion and press ideas.

With 40 percent of her time spent on phone calls, and 20 percent in travel, Jeri has a long workday. Although she tries to leave by 6:00 P.M., she has a computer and LaserJet printer at home. She often works weekends at home but generally won't come into the office. Her short-term goal: to free up time to do more product introduction planning.

Salary for a job in in-house public relations ranges from $28,000 to $45,000. Jobs at outside public relations often pay far more, because agencies with high-tech clients need very qualified public relations professionals. Although she does not have an M.B.A., she recommends that degree for someone who wants the business side of laser products. Her advice to young people starting out? "Don't be afraid to try things, even if they're outside your area of expertise. Stretch and risk a little in what you are doing."

Sales, marketing, public relations, dealer relations, promotion, and publicity; all these are nontechnical areas, Jeri says, but they're ideas in which people wanting work related to lasers can find enjoyment and careers.

HOLOGRAMS

The terms "hologram" and "holography" were coined in 1947 by Dennis Gabor, the "father of holography." The word "hologram" comes from the Greek words *holos* (meaning whole or complete) and *gram* (meaning message).

Holograms have been described as painting with light. That's not strictly true, of course, but to people who watch Dr. Tung H. Jeong, Albert Blake Dick Professor of physics at Lake Forest (Illinois) College and author of *Laser Holography: Experiments You Can Do,* it seems as if that's what he's doing. Magically, through using a simple laser and everyday objects, Jeong demonstrates that laser light can make a color picture on black and white film without a camera—a picture that can be seen with ordinary light.

The process looks simple. Yet, Jeong says, four separate Nobel prizes have been awarded for the theories contained in that one sentence.

In order to make the process easier to understand, Jeong uses what he calls the "soap bubble theory." He shows kids how, with water just from the sink, it's possible to produce beautiful soap bubbles with all the colors of the rainbow. It's the same theory, he says, that lies behind how we get holograms in color from black and white film.

How Lasers Make Holograms

When Jeong makes a hologram, he splits the laser beam in two with a lens. One of the two beams bounces off the object Jeong is using and is reflected back onto photographic film. The other beam from the laser hits the film directly, but doesn't bounce off the subject. Although both halves of the beam were coherent when they left the laser, they are no longer coherent when they reach the film. Some of the light waves that strike the film arrive in certain patterns, producing a double-strength wave called a *reinforcement*. Other waves show a pattern producing a *cancellation*. These patterns are recorded on the film. The resulting hologram can be used to reconstruct a three-dimensional picture of the object.

One of the most fascinating things about holograms is that you can cut up one of them into tiny pieces. Yet, unlike ordinary photographs, each small fragment contains a complete representation of the object.

How Holograms Are Used

You may be carrying a hologram right now. Just look at a credit card. If you see a multicolored three-dimensional image of the MasterCard or Visa logo, you have a transmission hologram. Actually, the embossed insignia really does not transmit light from the far side of the hologram, but the silvery backing fools the hologram into thinking it's doing so. Another common use of holograms, though you may not realize it, often happens at the supermarket check-out counter. The clerk passes one of your items over the scanner window. A spinning hologram under the counter locates the bar code on the product. The hologram directs the reflected light back from the bar code into the store's computer, which has been programmed to recognize the item and to enter its price on the cash register.

Corporations also use holograms as an attention-getter. Jeong himself was commissioned to photograph former Olympic gymnast Mary Lou Retton for possible use of the hologram by McDonald's, one of her sponsors. "We went to Salt Lake City for the project," Jeong recalls, "since I had a friend there with some special equipment." Retton was photographed with a light exposure of 1/20 billionth of a second, with a special lens under vibration-free conditions. Jeong created a similar photograph of Ronald McDonald, used in McDonald's annual franchise show at Las Vegas.

Holograms have many other uses. One that might not occur to you can be thought of as similar to time-lapse photography. As Jeong reported at a 1988 meeting of the International Society of Optical Engineers, once you've made a hologram, you can compare what you recorded with the living, and growing, object. For instance, he says, you can superimpose a hologram image of a mushroom on top of the growing fungus. You can measure the growth, second by second, as it grows in real-time—as you watch the differences between the static hologram and the living fungus.

This ability to compare recorded versus actual objects makes using holograms helpful in nondestructive testing. An aircraft tire can be recorded on a hologram and then inflated. If there is a defect in the tire, it will expand at a slightly larger rate than the rest of the tire. The trouble spot shows up, when compared to the baseline hologram.

Holograms can even show antimatter. Working with Jeong, scientists at Fermilab near Batavia, Illinois, have recorded bubbles formed in a liquefied hydrogen chamber—particles that exist for only 10^{-12} seconds. The bubbles that form for such a brief time can be photographed by laser light.

Information storage is another technology Jeong and other researchers are pioneering. One of his friends from China is able to record entire encyclopedias on a single sheet of film—pages that can be randomly accessed. With such a technology, it would be possible to store your entire personal medical record on a piece of plastic the size of a credit card.

Another application for holograms has been to record cultural treasures. Treasures from the Soviet Union and from the ancient civilization of Thrace have been photographed with laser light, and their resulting holograms are being sold as art objects. It was Soviet scientists, in fact, who worked out the process by which holograms are made that are visible under "normal" white light; a second kind of hologram, invented earlier, could only be viewed by laser light.

A HOLOGRAPHY ARTIST

Doris Vila is chair of the Department of Holography at the School of the Art Institute and herself an accomplished holographer. One of her latest commissioned holographic works is at the School of Nursing, University of Wisconsin–Eau Claire.

Vila, who says she "came at" holography from the artistic, rather than the scientific, side, became interested in the subject even before she saw her first hologram in 1979. "I wanted to know more," she remembers. Now, she views holography as an art form, rather than a revolution in imaging technology.

She explains holograms to students by asking them to imagine that you are "standing at the edge of a pond, throwing in a stone that generates wavelets out in circles. When you throw in a second stone, it too has circles of wavelets. At a certain point where wave crests generated from each stone meet, where crest meets crest, it gets higher, and where crest and trough meet, they cancel each other out. Imagine that we can make a small metal grating that captures the interference pattern. We'd insert it into the pond, and let everything go still again. Yet the grating would record those patterns."

As Vila explains, you can think of holograms as a tiny window (or the small grating in the pond). The information as to the stone's position is contained in a field over the holograph. It's not a specific point-to-point correspondence, as it would be in a photograph. That's why holograms are essentially a storage medium.

At the School of the Art Institute, in Chicago, courses are offered in beginning and in intermediate/advanced holography. Even the beginning course is a full semester of hands-on learning, in which students set up their own cameras, tune spatial filters, and work with their own personal imagery. Although the emphasis is on artistic results, students do study the structure of light, as well as the theory and techniques of three-dimensional imaging. If they wish, they can sign up for as many as twenty-four hours of lab time each week.

Advanced students gain a working knowledge of multi-image display holograms, as well as techniques for producing master holograms, both for white light transmission and reflection work.

Students in the M.F.A. program can emphasize holography.

"The School of the Art Institute has the most substantial art holography program in the United States," Vila says. Other resources she recommends include New York Holographic Labs and the Museum of Holography in New York City, as well as Chicago's Museum of Holography and a similar museum in Los Angeles—Holographic Visions.

Vila herself specializes in large-scale rainbow holography. "I work in a narrative style, combining photographs, shadowgrams, and stenciled imagery with found objects," she says. "What artists find quickly is that you need to learn the scientific principles behind holography in order to do better work. What photography taught us about how we see, holography can teach us about how we perceive."

CHAPTER 7

LASERS IN RESEARCH

There is a very strong link between laser research and its commercial applications. For example, the research facilities of Bell Labs are key sites of laser research. While most of the developments have a strong relevance to the commercial enterprise of Lucent Technologies, other wings of Bell Labs are engaged in research that is less immediately commercial.

Other scientists work in academic, scientific, and government facilities to discover new laser technologies and their uses.

TECHNOLOGY TRANSFER

Technology transfer—to and from military and space programs—is taking place in a number of locations, including the various military service research and development agencies, NASA centers, and federal laboratories. Here, significant advances in technology and recent inventions from the military programs are being studied. Scientists hope they will be able to use them commercially. Many of these items are already being produced by the private sector. Others will become new products of tomorrow.

Although the Strategic Defense Initiative (SDI) was never implemented as a defense weapon, the laser technology involved in SDI created a broad range of spin-offs. These can add up to significant benefits in terms of human welfare, industrial efficiency, and economic value.

Qualified American business and academic clients that have been approved under procedures established by the Department of Defense can learn about civil applications of this technology through using a referral database. Open to all federal and state agencies, the database is accessible through a computer modem. Technology application panels are being established in various areas, including biomedical applications; electronics, communications, and computer applications; power-generation, storage, and transmission applications; and materials and industrial process applications.

MEDICAL FREE-ELECTRON LASER PROGRAM

Since 1985 Congress has funded medical, biomedical, and materials research on free-electron laser technology. Regional medical free-electron laser research centers have been established at a number of facilities, including at Stanford University, the University of California at Santa Barbara, Brookhaven National Laboratory, the National Bureau of Standards (in Maryland), and Vanderbilt University.

In addition, preclinical medical research on surgical applications, therapy, and the diagnosis of disease is being conducted at, among other locations, the Massachusetts General Hospital, the University of Utah, Northwestern University, Baylor Medical School, and the University of California at Irvine. Biophysics research is being carried out at the University of Michigan, Purdue University, the University of Texas, Jackson Laboratories (Maine), and Physical Science (Massachusetts). Materials science is being investigated at Brown University, the State University of New

York at Buffalo, the University of Utah, and Stanford, Vanderbilt, Princeton, and Southern Methodist universities.

OTHER SPIN-OFF APPLICATIONS

Key examples of SDI technology that have found potential civil applications provide a substantial economic return on investment. They include optical computing, using laser light instead of electrical circuits for transmitting data; more efficient, less expensive electrical power systems; lightweight mirrors that can be aligned through computer control and used for lasers in manufacturing processes; and integration of laser technology, robotics, and computerized techniques for precision control into applications for manufacturing processes and biomedical work.

In addition, free-electron lasers have the potential for being used in noninvasive cancer surgery, early diagnosis and treatment of heart disease and stroke, and other medical diagnostic and treatment applications.

Scientists in the laboratories mentioned above are working hard at finding new and practical uses for lasers. You can learn more about what they are doing by writing to the public relations or press office of the universities and hospitals, asking to be put on the mailing list for copies of news releases mentioning lasers. Addresses for the universities can be found in reference books available at your school or public library and in inexpensive almanacs.

LASER FUSION

Research into laser fusion offers another career opportunity for working with lasers. If laser fusion energy can be commercially feasible, it could provide an environmentally safe form of energy that is virtually inexhaustible.

The sun generates its energy through thermonuclear fusion of hydrogen atoms. Fusion energy research on Earth is an effort to re-create and harness that energy. In the sun, gravity holds charged particles together in a tightly packed mass. That's why fusion reactions can occur on the sun at temperatures of about fourteen million degrees. But because the Earth has only a fraction of the sun's enormous gravity, scientists must create more extreme conditions in order to make fusion possible.

On the Earth the fuel density of a fusion reaction must be in the range of ten to twenty times that of lead, and temperatures must reach about fifty million degrees. When these conditions have been achieved, the fusion fuel undergoes a thermonuclear "burn." As a result, large amounts of energy are released—many times more energy than the laser beam emitted to start the reaction.

At the University of Rochester, in New York, the Laboratory for Laser Energetics uses a twelve-trillion watt OMEGA laser system to study the potential of high-powered lasers to produce controlled thermonuclear fusion. In order to do this, target pellets of fusion fuel must be heated and compressed so rapidly that the fusion fuel will burn before the highly compressed hot material flies apart. Powerful laser beams, split, amplified, and converted from infra-red light to ultraviolet (which is more effectively absorbed by the target pellets) are focused precisely on the pellets. When the beams hit the pellets, the surface matter blasts outward at a velocity of nearly six hundred miles per second. An equal force implodes on the shell containing the fuel. The kinetic energy of the imploding material is converted to heat.

The OMEGA laser is the size of a football field. The beams it emits arrive at the target within a millionth of a millionth of a second of one another at a spot defined by dimensions smaller than a tenth of the diameter of a human hair.

In 1988 scientists at Rochester reported they'd achieved a major milestone by using the OMEGA laser to compress and heat a small capsule of fusion fuel to the highest density achieved that has ever been directly measured—in the range of two to four times that of lead, with a temperature in the range of five to ten million degrees. The fusion fuel was compressed to a density more than one hundred times its normal liquid density. If you could compress water to the same degree, an eight-ounce glass would weigh about fifty pounds. A gallon of water, compressed to the same degree as the fusion fuel in the laser experiments, would weigh nearly half a ton.

Sophisticated technology allows the scientists to split each of OMEGA's twenty-four laser beams into several thousand beams that strike the target simultaneously. The target pellets are glass shells about the size of a grain of sand containing a frozen layer of fusion fuel. In order to compress the pellets evenly and prevent an area on their surface from "ballooning out," the laser must irradiate the entire surface of the spherical fuel pellets with a high degree of uniformity. Splitting the beams so they strike the fuel pellets simultaneously lets the laser do this.

The burst of energy from the OMEGA laser that compresses and heats fusion fuel is incredibly short. The blast of laser light lasts about .6 of a nanosecond (6/10th of a billionth of a second). For that period of time the OMEGA laser is twenty times brighter than the peak generating capacity of all the electrical generating plants in the United States.

Additional research in laser fusion is being conducted at Lawrence Livermore National Laboratory, Livermore, California. Scientists there are using the extremely large Nova laser for similar inertial confinement experiments.

LASER ISOTOPE SEPARATION

Scientists at the Lawrence Livermore National Laboratory are also using lasers to separate isotopes in order to increase the concentration of valuable forms of the elements uranium and plutonium. Their goal is to help keep the price of American enriched uranium competitive with the price charged by foreign companies.

In its natural state uranium is a mixture of two isotopes: U-235 and U-238. But U-235 amounts to only about 0.7 percent of natural uranium by weight. Uranium used as fuel in a nuclear reactor must have 3 percent of U-235. Consequently, natural uranium must be enriched.

Because different uranium isotopes absorb light tuned to different wavelengths, laser light—precisely tuned to desired wavelengths—separates the isotopes. The system uses two types of lasers: dye lasers that generate the light used for photoionization of the uranium, and copper-vapor lasers that energize the dye lasers. Powerful green-yellow light from the copper-vapor lasers is converted to red-orange light in the dye laser. This red-orange light is tuned to the precise colors that are absorbed by U-235 but not by U-238.

In the Livermore project, uranium is heated in a vacuum chamber. A set of laser beams, tuned to wavelengths that match those of the desired U-235 atoms, passes through the vapor. When the atoms absorb the laser light, they pick up enough energy to give up one of their negatively charged electrons. The U-235 atoms—now positively charged—are pulled from the vapor by an electric field and become enriched uranium, which can be made into fuel to drive nuclear power reactors. The U-238 atoms, which don't have an electrical charge, pass through the electric field and onto a collector.

CONTRACT RESEARCH

Not all research with lasers is taking place at universities. Typical, perhaps, of the type of arrangement possible between industry and a research partner is the contract between the Gas Research Institute, an industry trade association, and SRI, a consulting group from Palo Alto, California. Current technology used in detecting gas leaks is based upon a flame ionization device. The laser-based leak detector SRI is developing, however, may reduce labor costs for leak surveys by as much as 50 percent, as well as improve pipeline safety.

"We put out a competitive Request for Proposals (RFP)," says Dr. Tom Altpeter, research manager, environment and safety, at Gas Research Institute. "We were testing the technical market-place of ideas to see if we could find something better than exist-ing technology."

What GRI wanted was a detector that would be selective for ethane (natural gas)—a detector that would ignore methane pro-duced by swamp gas, or gas from automobile exhausts.

As Altpeter explains, the device, when tested and operational, will find natural gas leaks from buried pipes in the street or gas mains. The laser will be mounted on a van, which can be driven at speeds up to thirty miles per hour. As the laser beam sweeps the street, at a distance up to 150 feet ahead of the van, its beams fan out, becoming divergent, rather than being compressed into the more common, threadlike laser beams. The carbon dioxide laser, which normally operates around the ten micrometer range, has been converted to the three micrometer range, which is selective for ethane and ignores other gases.

Light from the laser is reflected back to special receiving devices on the van. If the laser light senses ethane, however, it's preferen-tially absorbed by the leaking gas. Careful measurements, built in as part of the device, show the difference between the light the device has sent out and the light reflected back when ethane is present.

LASER RESEARCH AT BATTELLE

At Battelle Memorial Institute, more than 8,000 scientists, engi-neers, economists, and supporting specialists conduct more than 6,000 studies per year, with an annual business volume of $958 million. Much of this work is done by Battelle under contract from industrial organizations and government agencies.

Laser research at Battelle-Columbus is handled by a special laser technology group. In an assortment of programs, Battelle is developing applications of high-powered CO_2 laser radiation for welding, cutting, transformation hardening, and cladding of metals. In addition, lasers are being studied for improvements in cutting, shaping, and thermal processing of glasses and ceramics.

"At Battelle, we're working with low-powered and high-powered lasers," says Dr. Frank Jacoby, principal research scientist. A "sensor group" is researching applications for solid-state and He:Ne lasers. At Battelle, other scientists run a CO_2 laser lab in which industrial research is carried on.

Battelle scientists also are studying two types of Nd-doped lasers: an Nd:YAG laser, which is used for testing various industrial processes, and an Nd: glass laser. "One of our laser scientists believes that by using modern glass and making the laser beam very long and thin that we can achieve the same thermal performance as we do with the Nd:YAG laser," explains Jacoby.

Another laser project at Battelle focuses on laser shock hardening. When a laser beam is shot into metal, it can make the metal sixty times stronger, Jacoby says. That idea has gone beyond the testing stage; one Battelle scientist has received a patent, and metal companies are working with Battelle to commercialize the process.

JOBS IN RESEARCH

Research scientists who work with lasers have challenging careers. On the one hand, they have the knowledge that puts them on the frontier of technology; on the other hand, funding for R&D projects is often dependent on outside sources, such as Congress or private companies. Consequently, how many jobs there will be and who will get (and keep) them may depend on how successful the laboratory is at coming up with proposals or landing contracts.

One way to learn about such jobs is by reading the trade publications. For instance, a postdoctoral position in ultra-fast laser spectroscopy at Hampton University in Hampton, Virginia, was recently advertised in *Optics and Photonics News,* published by the Optical Society of America. This publication also carries employment listings for laser-related positions in the military and business, as well as for international academic and research positions.

In order to qualify for these, and other positions, candidates should have a doctor's or a master's degree in physics, electrical engineering, or mechanical engineering. In addition, they should be experienced in such fields as quantum optics, atmospheric physics, optical engineering, image and signal processing, or circuit design.

SECURITY CLEARANCE

Because many research laboratories are working on government-funded projects, U.S. citizenship is generally a requirement for employment. In addition, your personal record should generally meet any requirements for obtaining security clearance. Laboratories are generally equal opportunity employers and welcome applications from qualified candidates, regardless of sex or minority background. Salaries are competitive, and benefits are generally comprehensive.

In labs like Battelle, entry-level jobs for laser technicians require a two-year program in technology, according to Jacoby. Typically, the technician runs the equipment. The next level up, for Battelle, is that of laser researcher—a man or woman who often runs experiments as well as doing day-to-day laser operations. Most researchers Battelle hires have a four-year degree; however,

Battelle recently promoted one laser technician who attended Ohio State University (with tuition help from Battelle) and who received the bachelor's degree.

Next highest position? Project researcher, if you're managing projects. Generally, the master's degree is the prerequisite. Persons like Jacoby, who have a Ph.D., can become a research scientist, who is basically in charge of medium-sized projects or handles a certain subsection of a major project.

Jacoby says that unlike company labs in which defense contracting plays a major role, Battelle doesn't require U.S. citizenship and often employs a number of foreign nationals. "That's because we have so many projects happening simultaneously," he explains.

A LASER RESEARCH SCIENTIST

One of the roles Jacoby finds himself playing is that of fundraiser. "At Battelle, principal research scientists like me are essentially people who get ideas, think up projects, and then go out and try to find people to pay for them," he explains. "For instance, I have the CO_2 laser lab. In our laser paint-stripping research, we run tests, and then we try to find people who want to strip paint."

Jacoby's days usually start at 8:30 A.M. and end at 5:30 P.M., though in research labs, he says, the hours are somewhat flexible. On the days he meets visitors and nonlab personnel, he dresses in a suit and tie; "If I'm down messing with the equipment," he says, "I come in wearing grungies. What I wear depends on my schedule."

A typical day found Jacoby helping to host a visiting group from a tractor company interested in laser robotics. Though the group spent the entire day at Battelle, he spoke with them for about two hours, leading them on a tour of his part of the facilities. Two or three more hours that day were spent in writing proposals and in catching up with his correspondence. Later he helped troubleshoot in another lab, assisting the scientists there to solve problems on their project and arranging for equipment to be built for their future needs.

Although Battelle has no hard-and-fast rule, Jacoby says, roughly 40 percent of his time "should" be spent in marketing Battelle's services. That might involve travel to prospective companies that might fund projects or arrange for Battelle to do contract research.

Salaries for scientists at his level, he says, range between $50,000 and $70,000—higher on the coasts, because of the cost-of-living difference. Jacoby says that senior research scientists in laboratories might earn more than $90,000.

His advice to young people who want to work with laser research: look for universities or hospitals with laboratories and get hired at the technician level. Ohio State University has a research foundation similar to Battelle's, he says, in which companies with a problem can hire a team headed by an OSU professor to work on it. Such a lab affiliated with a university is a good source of openings for laser technicians, Jacoby says. "It's a good way to start in the laser area."

CHAPTER 8

PREPARING FOR A CAREER
IN LASER TECHNOLOGIES

The opportunity to work in a job that utilizes laser technology has never been greater. Lasers have become an integral part of manufacturing, medicine, communications, and dozens of other fields. Be that as it may, it is highly unlikely that you can just turn to the want ads in your Sunday newspaper and just scan for jobs in lasers! Careers in laser technology are arrived at by many paths, and you will most likely find your path by preparing for a career in a field that appeals to you on a number of levels. Perhaps you are drawn to the prospect of helping people recover from illnesses or accidents, and will find a career working with lasers in health care, whether as a doctor, ophthalmologist's assistant, nurse, or laser technician. Or maybe you are happiest when working alone in a research setting, and will be looking for employment in a university or commercial research laboratory. You might even find your place as a holographic or laser light show artist! Whatever route you take, be certain that the challenges of working with lasers require a strong mind for detail and a passion for learning new techniques, as laser technology is sure to be developing rapidly.

SCIENCE LITERACY

Working in laser technology calls for a solid understanding of the mathematical and scientific principles at work in lasers. The more math and science competency you develop, the better equipped you will be when faced with the complex concepts of physics and optics involved in laser technology. You can even start preparing for your future in lasers while still in junior high school by taking any extra math and science classes that are offered at your school. Even though you may not be working in an area directly related to lasers, the additional scientific and mathematical training will serve you well in the future.

In fact, there is a great push in the United States to try and improve science literacy. A person who is science literate is someone who understands that science, math, and technology are interdependent human enterprises, each with its own benefits and drawbacks. Science literacy also calls for an understanding of key concepts and principles of science, as well as a familiarity with the diversity and unity of the natural world. Finally, someone who is science literate uses scientific knowledge for his or her individual and social purposes.

In 1996, the American Association for the Advancement of Science (AAAS), the National Academy of Sciences, and the National Science Teachers Association released a joint statement announcing their commitment to science literacy for all Americans. The drive for greater science literacy began in 1985, when the AAAS began a long-term project aimed at changing the way that science, math, and technology was taught in schools in the United States. That same year, Halley's comet was in view. The panel of experts at the AAAS considered how many scientific and technological changes a child just beginning school in 1985 would see before Halley's comet returned in 2061. Would he or she be prepared to understand, contribute to, and benefit from the changes that lay ahead?

The experts, who included scientists, mathematicians, and technologists, decided to launch what they called Project 2061 to establish guidelines for science literacy. Project 2061 produced two significant reports: "Science for All Americans" (1990) and "Benchmarks for Science Literacy" (1993). These important reports reviewed the state of American scientific literacy and challenged the established methods of teaching science by creating a coherent set of specific learning goals for elementary, middle, and high school students. These benchmarks were instrumental in shaping the National Science Education Standards, which are used by school districts throughout the United States to create science and mathematics curricula. The Project 2061 experts also examined how science should best be taught. They determined that teaching science required more time than had traditionally been assumed. Students need time to explore, make observations, test ideas, build and refine projects and experiments, and even make mistakes in the process of gaining scientific knowledge. The process of truly coming to understand new concepts can not be rushed, the experts say, and must be presented periodically in different settings and at increasingly sophisticated levels of difficulty.

As the process of fostering scientific literacy throughout the country moves forward, what can you do to ensure that you are well-trained in the basic principles? The most direct answer is to enroll in the widest range of science and math classes available at your junior high and high school. If you are not in one of the larger school districts, where courses might include physics and calculus, it may be possible for you to register for courses at a magnet school or technical high school. You may even find that it is possible to sign-up for classes at a local community college, where there is usually open enrollment.

If you think you want to work with lasers, you will have to take an active role in your own education. You will need to work closely with guidance counselors, math and science teachers, and other school personnel to be sure that you benefit from every opportunity. There may be special exams to take to qualify for a magnet school or a technical high school. A teacher or counselor may be willing to give you extra coaching or tutoring so you can do well on the exams. They might even plan extra assignments or suggested projects for you to complete outside of class. If you have demonstrated an eagerness to advance your knowledge, you will no doubt find allies who are willing to go to bat for you. These allies can put you in touch with a faculty member from a nearby college or university, or perhaps can help you arrange to visit someone who is working with lasers.

Although you will want to extend yourself in science and math, it is important not to neglect the other academic subjects. You will want to do well in your English classes, as communication skills are crucial to your success, especially when you are called upon to write reports and make presentations. And clearly you will want to become very proficient in using computers, as they are often inextricably linked with laser technologies.

The Optical Society of America, a society of more than twelve-thousand scientists, engineers, and entrepreneurs in a wide array of disciplines and industries (many of whom work directly with lasers), has a number of educational options for students. These include the OSA Optics Discovery Kit, which is targeted at grades six through nine but is often used for projects at the elementary level as well as in university courses. The kit features eleven experiments that demonstrate the basic principles of optics, including lenses, optical fibers, a hologram, and an optical illusion slide. The Optics Discover Kits are distributed by Edmund Scientific Company, a scientific products firm that also distributes scientific apparatuses such as lasers, beam splitters, measuring devices, teaching aids, and other fascinating educational tools, as well as general science items. You can get more information by writing to Edmund Scientific Company, Industrial Operations Division, 101 East

Gloucester Pike, Barrington, NJ 08007-1380. The telephone number is (609) 573-6250; web site: www.edsci.com.

The OSA also produces a twenty-minute video on lasers. This video traces the history of the laser and demonstrates "the characteristics of diode, solid-state, and gas lasers, and the properties that make them useful in a variety of applications, from welding to fiber optics to CD players." This video can be obtained directly from the Optical Society of America, 2010 Massachusetts Avenue NW, Washington, DC 20036-1023. The phone number for OSA customer service is (202) 416-1907; web site: www.osa.org. The cost is $25.00; discounts are available for larger orders.

COLLEGE AND BEYOND

Colleges and universities change with the times, offering degrees in subjects that weren't even dreamt of merely a decade ago. Specialized programs in optics, the field that encompasses laser technology, are just one example of the ways that institutions of advanced learning adapt and grow. In 1960, when the laser was first invented, research into lasers was conducted from within physics or engineering departments. By the turn of the century, laser-based optical systems are omnipresent—in CD players, laser bar code scanners, hospital surgery rooms, and telecommunications centers. As lasers have moved into every corner of our lives, colleges and universities have developed specialized programs for undergraduate, graduate, postdoctoral, and continuing education in optical science and engineering.

At many universities, programs in optics continue to be housed within physics or electrical engineering departments. However, some schools have established comprehensive programs offering degrees in optics as a separate discipline. Whether you obtain your college or graduate degree in optics from a physics department or from a separate optical sciences department, you will most likely be trained in the wide range of the field, from fundamental through applied science to engineering. That said, if you study in a traditional science department like physics, you will find that this discipline tends to stress the scientific aspect of optics rather than the applications. Should you study at a program that is part of an electrical engineering department, you will find the emphasis to be more on how the technology is applied. The specialized optics programs, on the other hand, tend to spread the focus out, encompassing fundamental and applied subjects equally. The faculty for the specialized programs are drawn from a variety of specialties, including physics, engineering, and materials science. Most of these programs are designed for graduate study, so it will be necessary to get your undergraduate science degree first.

"If you want to do graduate study in optics and lasers, any good university with a good program in physics or electrical engineering can prepare you," says Dr. M. J. Soileau, who heads CREOL—the University of Central Florida's Center for Research and Education in Optics and Lasers. "You really need a solid background in either physics or applied physics. You need a very strong math background, starting with calculus. As a college undergraduate, take as much math as you can, at the highest level of sophistication possible. The more you're proficient in math, the easier it is to do the science and the engineering. A good background in physics and engineering—preferably electrical engineering—will help you if you want to do laser research."

UNIVERSITY OF ROCHESTER

The Laboratory for Laser Energetics, a multidisciplinary teaching and research unit of the College of Engineering and Applied Science at the University of Rochester, is the first of its kind at any

American college or university. Students are involved in all of the research programs, including a project to explore the potential of high-powered lasers to produce controlled thermonuclear fusion as an alternative energy source. The laboratory's principal research tool is a twelve-trillion-watt laser system, the world's most powerful UV laser. At the laboratory, research activities include major programs in photo-matter interactions, optical materials development, laser physics and technology, and the physics of ultrahigh density phenomena.

The laboratory contains the new Ultrafast Science Center, which investigates the production and utilization of phenomena occurring on time scales of less than a billionth of a second.

Undergraduate students who want to concentrate in engineering are assigned faculty advisers in the College of Engineering and Applied Science in their freshman year. They may (and usually do) begin taking engineering courses as early as their first semester.

During their first two years, they receive a strong liberal arts education. In the spring of their sophomore year students apply formally to the College of Engineering and Applied Science by filing a "concentration approval" form in which they list an approved plan of study for their last two years.

A special five-year program is available for electrical engineering juniors who contemplate graduate work. Students are accepted into this program in the spring of their junior year and can begin master's level independent work in their senior year. At the end of the five-year program, both a bachelor's and master's degrees in electrical engineering are awarded.

Institute of Optics

The Institute of Optics at the University of Rochester is an internationally known center for teaching and research. The institute offers programs of study leading to the B.S., M.S., and Ph.D.

degrees in optics. Optics majors who plan to do graduate work may apply in their junior year for admission to the five-year B.S.-M.S. program.

Students normally apply for admission to the Institute of Optics at the end of the sophomore year by submitting a concentration approval form. Certain prerequisite courses and certain minimum cumulative and specific grade point averages are required.

Interested and qualified undergraduates often are able to take part in faculty research projects during the school year or in the summer. Research programs in the Institute of Optics cover the fundamental-to-applied continuum, including imaging, lasers, optical materials, optics manufacturing, semiconductor lasers, theoretical foundations, ultrafast phenomena, and diffractive-fiber, gradient-index, guided-wave, nonlinear, and quantum optics.

The Institute of Optics is home to the Laboratory for Laser Energetics, the Center for Electronic Imaging Systems, and the Center for Optics Manufacturing.

Prospective students and undergraduates considering optics as a major are encouraged to write or to visit The Institute of Optics, University of Rochester, Rochester, NY 14627. The web site for the institute is: www.optics.rochester.edu.

UNIVERSITY OF ARIZONA

At the University of Arizona, Tucson, the Optical Sciences Center is a graduate center for research and teaching in optical sciences and engineering, and is one of only three places in the United States where students can obtain a comprehensive education in all areas of optics, leading to an M.S. or Ph.D. in Optical Sciences, or (in collaboration with Electrical Engineering) a B.S. in Optical Engineering.

There were 50 faculty members and more than 140 graduate students in 1999. The center's research program and course offerings cover the entire range of optical science, from fundamental optical physics and the development of new optical and electrooptical devices, to lens design and optical system engineering. It has numerous laboratories as well as equipment used for research in a broad range of optics.

Interdisciplinary programs currently involve the departments of Astronomy, Chemistry, Civil Engineering and Engineering Mechanics, Electrical and Computer Engineering, Microbiology, Physics, Physiology, Planetary Sciences, and Radiology.

Several faculty members have specialties in laser work—including laser system application, laser spectroscopy and laser spectroscopy of solids, holographic techniques, laser physics, pulse propagation in laser amplifiers and attenuators, short-pulse production in lasers, high-energy lasers, and laser amplifiers.

Says faculty member Dr. Frederic A. Hopf, "While second-harmonic generation of high-power pulsed lasers and low-power continuous-wave lasers is a well-developed technology, little is known about high average-power applications.

"The ultimate goal of one of our research projects is the development of high-power (more than one kilowatt) single-mode visible lasers.

"Our free-electron laser (FEL) project has concentrated on an investigation into the nature of short-pulse traveling-wave amplification."

At the Optical Sciences Center, work on laser analysis has included development of computer models of laser fusion, laser isotope separation, free-electron lasers, and other complex laser systems. The free-electron laser model was the first three-dimensional, time-dependent treatment and included detailed interactions between the optical and electron beams.

Dr. George N. Lawrence, associate professor, describes one OSC research project as "studying the design and performance of optical data storage read/write heads, which consist of a laser diode, a slab waveguide, and a chirped grating to couple from the waveguide mode out to a focused spot."

Interested students should write to the Optical Sciences Center, the University of Arizona, Tucson, Arizona, 85721-0094. The web site is www.opt-sci.arizona.edu.

UNIVERSITY OF CENTRAL FLORIDA

One major center for graduate students is the UCF Center for Research and Education in Optics and Lasers (CREOL)—an interdisciplinary center formed to provide direct access by Florida's high-tech industry to UCF's program in electro-optics. Faculty members from the departments of electrical engineering, physics, math, and mechanical engineering work with the program, along with a board of directors that includes several prominent representatives of local industry. Florida has one of the largest concentrations of electro-optic industrial activity in the United States, with some fifteen laser companies in Orlando alone.

CREOL is one of the three independent academic optics departments in the United States and offers master's and doctoral degrees in optics, photonics, and laser sciences and engineering. In 1999 the program had twenty-five full-time faculty members, as well as twenty-five Ph.D.-level research scientists.

Research is an integral part of CREOL. Soileau and several faculty members are studying nonlinear optics, including a project on how very high-powered laser radiation interacts with materials. Related projects include using high-intensity light to do optical switching—studies that may have eventual application to optical computing and optical information processing. "In addition," says

Soileau, "our studies can lead to defense applications that help protect people from deliberate or inadvertent exposure to lasers. This work involves a variety of different kinds of lasers. With pulse lasers, short pulses act as clocks like a strobe light to stop or study the details of very fast processes in nature."

Another CREOL faculty member is using various kinds of crystals to change the color of laser light—research that may have medical implications. "You may have the type of tumor that absorbs light preferentially at one wavelength," Soileau explains. "So you want to tune the laser to that wavelength. This project is attempting to come up with new laser sources that can be tuned over a large span of wavelengths, but can be compact and economical. Although we currently can make tunable lasers, they tend to be extremely large. We need new sources for smaller tunable lasers."

CREOL provides students with a wide array of extra opportunities to pursue their research and professional goals. There are active student chapters of the Optical Society of America (OSA), the IEEE-Lasers and Electro-Optics Society (IEEE-LEOS), and the International Society for Optical Engineering (SPIE). And one of the more impressive features of CREOL is the new eighty-two-thousand-square-foot facility specifically designed for research and education in optics, photonics, and laser sciences and engineering.

For information write to CREOL, University of Central Florida, 4000 Central Florida Boulevard, Orlando, FL 32816-2700. The web site address is: www.creol.ucf.edu.

A Laser Research Project

The story of Edesly Canto, a graduate student from Panama, illustrates what it is like to work with lasers on a research project.

Edesly brings a rich and varied background to her studies. By the time she finished six years of elementary school in Panama, she qualified through examinations and high grades for a science high school. In her six years there she studied chemistry, biology, and mathematics and took several levels of physics classes as well. By the time she graduated she was fluent in Spanish, Portuguese, and English. She enrolled in Southeastern Oklahoma University, Durant, Oklahoma, and earned a bachelor's degree in physics, with minors in chemistry and math. During her studies she did a number of optics experiments that involved small lasers. She studied dispersion properties of lasers and learned how lasers work.

Next, she became a teaching assistant at North Texas State University. She completed her master's degree in 1985 and became research assistant to Dr. Soileau, then a North Texas State Professor. When Soileau moved to Orlando to head up CREOL, Edesly came along. She had finished her academic work for a Ph.D. at North Texas State and will receive her doctorate from that university after her CREOL research project and dissertation have been completed and approved.

At CREOL Edesly studies nonlinear properties of semiconductors, using zinc selenite. "We're trying to study the decay parameters and transport phenomena for this material," she explains, "so we can determine zinc selenite's physical constants. Once we know the constants, we will know how zinc selenite will behave under radiation from the atmosphere. We will know whether it can be used for windows on jets and other aircraft."

Edesly works with lasers daily, using the laser as a tool to study zinc selenite. "The Nd:YAG laser is a picosecond pulsed laser," she says. "I work in a time scale of picoseconds—one millionth of a second. By probing the sample of zinc selenite with this kind of time scale, we can study its microscopic properties. The pulses of the laser are so short that we can model what is happening in the sample."

The laser Edesly uses looks like a black box about five feet long and two feet wide. Most of the box is hollow to protect the actual path of the laser light from being scattered around. Even though the light itself can't be seen, since it is not in the visible part of the spectrum, Edesly and other CREOL researchers must wear special goggles to protect their eyes. She puts a special kind of crystal in the path of one of the laser beams to produce a light of exactly 1.06 microns. The light coming out of the laser is approximately 2 millimeters in diameter, but Edesly can compress or enlarge the beam for different experiments.

Each morning she arrives around 8:30 or 9:00 A.M. She turns on the laser power supply, which applies voltage to the flashlamps that optically prompt the material inside the laser. "The next thing I do is check the pulse of the laser," she says. "I want it to be the right width in time—about thirty picoseconds. I want the shape to be Gaussian—a shape that looks round to your eyes, but if you scan it in space, it looks like the bell curve used in statistics. I check the energy of the laser beam to be sure it meets my standards of four millijoules in energy. All this must be done each day and takes about an hour to complete."

Edesly's particular experiment probes the zinc selenite material with three different laser beams, all coming from the same Nd:YAG laser. "I use special mirrors," she explains. "Just by setting the laser in different positions I can make the beam go wherever necessary. Consequently, I need to check the alignment of all my optical mirrors, making sure all beams overlap at the sample. Once they do, I observe my conjugate beam, which is the product of the overlapping of the three beams. By setting that fourth (or conjugate) beam I can get all the information necessary for my data.

"I can change the energy of each beam independently, if I like, by having an attenuator in each beam line. That's a combination of a linear polarizer and a halfway plate."

All this is computerized, she explains. Edesly has detectors that are connected to a microcomputer that makes the measurements.

She learned computer skills first as an undergraduate at Southeastern Oklahoma, but she took most of her computer courses at

North Texas State University. "Although I have help from many people," she says, "we do have to modify the software we need for our work. We also need to write all the plotting." Edesly uses Pascal (a computer language) for most of her work, but when she needs to go on UCF's mainframe computer for a long program, she uses FORTRAN, another computer language.

It's extremely important, Edesly says, to know the safety regulations for working with lasers and to follow them exactly. If she's working with liquid crystals she wears a lab coat; otherwise she dresses in comfortable clothing. She always wears goggles when working with lasers, and if she is handling chemicals, she wears rubber gloves. Her workday depends on what she needs to get done for her particular experiment. Sometimes she spends ten or eleven hours at the lab, and frequently she works on weekends.

When she finishes the requirements for her Ph.D., Edesly hopes to teach solid-state physics and optics at a university and to be involved in research as well. She'd rather work in lasers at a university than in industry, she says, but she believes the field is wide open. "Lasers are demanding and fascinating," she says. "There's so much more to learn. We're really just beginning to understand them. There's plenty of opportunity."

CHAPTER 9

JOB HUNTING STRATEGIES

Opportunities abound for those who seek a career in laser technologies. The prevalence of laser technologies in so many industries calls for growing numbers of trained, dedicated laser professionals. You will, of course, need to be trained properly in the science of lasers, as well as in the particulars of the industry that you choose to enter. But whatever route you follow, your search for a career in this field begins with a self-assessment of your own personal qualities.

PERSONAL CHARACTERISTICS

What type of person will succeed in a career with lasers? For starters, one who is enthusiastic about math and science. "So much of laser work is related to math and science that you really need to enjoy those fields," says Jack Dyer, communications director of the Laser Institute of America, one of the major laser associations. "The more you understand the optical and mathematical principles behind laser operation, the more chance you have to move ahead in the field, rather than merely running the machinery. You can go much further in your career."

It is also important to be able to follow directions precisely. The highly technical nature of working with lasers requires reading and understanding directions exactly and following them to the letter every time. Lasers are unforgiving; if you violate safety standards even once, you risk permanent damage. Various lasers require different types of protective eyewear. And just because you have gained previous experience with one type of laser does not mean that the same safety standards will automatically work with another. In one well-publicized case, a research scientist wearing inappropriate eyewear, while trying to look into the path of a Nd:YAG laser, received a retinal burn after fewer than thirty seconds of exposure.

To succeed in laser technology, especially at the level of technician, you also must be willing to accept responsibility. In a manufacturing plant you might be one of a handful of laser technicians—or indeed the only technician—among a large number of other workers or machinists. If the equipment breaks down, you've got to get it up and running, no matter what it takes. That may involve trying various ways to repair the machine yourself, contacting manufacturers for assistance, or working with plant engineers. The burden of getting the process back in motion may well rest entirely upon your shoulders.

No matter what your training has been, you will almost certainly find working with lasers to be an ongoing learning experience. As Dyer puts it, "You certainly won't be finished with your training when you graduate!" You will need to work on a variety of equipment, and you will gain hands-on experience at the plant or laser site. And as new techniques and uses for laser develop, you will be required to keep up with changes in the field through course work, seminars, after-hours study, reading the trade publications, and similar activities.

Only you can determine whether you truly have the aptitude and personal qualities necessary for a role in this demanding, challenging field. By being honest with yourself about your goals and abilities, you will have a far greater chance of finding yourself in a career that you truly enjoy. And your self-assessment also will help you to determine where in the vast field of laser technology you can make your best contribution.

"The laser field is broad enough so there's plenty of room for different personality types," says Dr. Frank Jacoby, principal research scientist at Battelle Laboratories in Columbus, Ohio. "If you're the kind of person who likes to sit in the backroom and play with equations, there's plenty of opportunity for that. If you're a social sort of person who wants to heal people and interact with patients, the whole medical laser field is wide open. And if you're interested in management and the business side of lasers, you can find jobs there also. So many little laser companies are starting up that you can essentially do almost any kind of work there."

As Jacoby summarizes, there are niches in laser jobs, niches enough to accommodate many types of people. "Laser technology is a much more open field than many others, in which everything is narrowed down and stratified—in which you're either one of 'them' or not," he explains.

So how do you go about finding your niche? What, realistically, are your chances of working with lasers? As someone just entering the field, you are probably going to hold another job within an organization before you are promoted to working directly with the lasers. The laser represents an enormous investment on the part of the company, so it is unlikely that a beginning technician will get "turned loose" to play with the company's very expensive machine. Instead, a department head is far more likely to promote from within—giving someone already employed by the organization the first chance at working with the laser.

BE SELECTIVE ABOUT YOUR TRAINING

Although there are many factors that will influence your chances for success in a laser career, there are certainly strategies you can use to get yourself in a better position. One of them is to be selective about the training you receive. You can find extensive course listings on the web site for SPIE—the International Society for Optical Engineering (www.spie.org). The programs include short courses and symposia as well as more in-depth programs. You also can request the SPIE educational catalog by writing to SPIE, P.O. Box 10, Bellingham, WA 98227-0010.

When considering colleges, choose carefully. Study their academic programs closely to make sure that they will provide you with the right level of training. Ask about their placement rate for graduates, especially for those who've taken course work in laser technology. Perhaps they will give you the names of one or two alumni in your area whom you can write to or phone. Persons who have studied lasers and who are now working in the field can give you invaluable advice about the preparation you should have and the current job market.

When you do enroll for course work, choose a school or technology program accredited by the Accreditation Board for Engineering and Technology (ABET). You can get a list from the board by writing the organization at 111 Market Place, Suite 1050, Baltimore, MD 21202. The telephone number is (410) 347-7700. The web site for the ABET, at www.abet.org, also contains complete listings of accredited schools and institutes. While graduation from an ABET-approved school or course of instruction is certainly not an automatic entry requirement for laser jobs, ABET thinks of itself as responsible for the "quality control for engineering education" and closely monitors the educational environment in the institutions it accredits.

During your school years, become active in local chapters of professional societies (see Appendix A). Writing to the national headquarters of those listed will put you on the mailing list for information. Ask to be placed in contact with the appropriate local chapter. Attending meetings regularly will help you learn more about lasers and will give you a chance to talk with professionals employed in the field.

Read three or four of the periodicals listed in Appendix B of this book; if possible, subscribe to them. Not only will you keep up with technological developments, but you also will learn dates of future conferences and seminars. Try to attend these. Often fees for students are extremely low, or waived with a letter from one of your professors. At these meetings you'll find vendors of various laser products. Pick up catalogs and information literature as well as business cards of company representatives. Some of them may be willing to talk with you about laser jobs and possible employment. Or they may know of customers—laser users—who are expanding and who are hiring.

Reading the trade periodicals will give you a list of vendors whom you can contact for literature, so you can keep up with new laser developments. Each year, several publications run a *Buyers Guide,* which includes company addresses. In addition, you can check your school or public library for reference publications listing lasers and laser services.

ON-LINE RESOURCES

Going on-line will be one of the most informative as well as enjoyable ways to keep up to date on current developments in laser technology. Nearly every organization, company, or school involved with lasers maintains an Internet web site. Many of these sites are quite elaborate, with in-depth explanations of research projects, technical innovations, and commercial applications. For example, the web site for Bell Laboratories, at www.bell-labs.com, will provide you with a wealth of information on current investigations in photonics and other laser-related research. The Lucent Technologies web site (www.lucent.com) provides an excellent array of information related to the commercial applications of technologies developed at Bell Labs. Another commercial site is that of the magazine *Laser Focus World,* at www.lfw.com. *Laser Focus World* publishes annual reviews and forecasts of the laser industry, and you will be able to locate very relevant career information on this site.

The web sites for the professional organizations provide valuable information on educational offerings, conferences, and professional publications. The Society of Manufacturing Engineers (www.sme.org) allows browsers to search by keyword through the thousands of publications indexed on their site. The web sites for OSA (www.osa.org) and SPIE (www.spie.org) are loaded with helpful information. And you can find information on lasers in medicine by visiting the web site for the American Society for Laser Medicine and Surgery (www.aslms.org). You probably will also want to visit the home page of the Laser Institute (www.laserinstitute.org), where you will find many useful links to laser organizations, manufacturers, and researchers.

Other fascinating sources of information on the World Wide Web include the web pages of the Department of Defense. Find out all about the various laser programs by searching at the DOD's web site, www.defenselink.mil.

RESUMES

When you're job-hunting, whether you're a beginner or experienced, highlight significant accomplishments. If you've achieved academic honors, list them. Instead of merely writing down on your resume the titles of courses you've had, however, indicate the types of laboratory or industrial equipment you've operated, including the types of lasers. Since many laser systems are computer controlled, put down your computer literacy—what hardware you've worked with or what computer languages you're fluent in.

If you've worked for only one company, summarize your experience. Be prepared to capsulize it by listing the two or three most significant things you've done.

Don't get discouraged if you don't get hired immediately by the company of your choice—or even by any company working with lasers. "Many companies and managers keep the resumes our placement firm submits," says Rudzinsky. "They stockpile them. When R&D dollars come in or a contract shows up, they know whom they're interested in interviewing."

SALARIES

What can you expect to earn in lasers? Detailed results on engineering salaries are available from the American Association of Engineering Societies (AAES). You can visit their web site (www.aaes.org) or write the AAES Engineering Workforce Commission, 1111 Nineteenth Street NW, Suite 403, Washington, DC 20036. These reports, however, can cost up to $100, so it is best to check with your local college or university library to see if they carry them in their reference department.

Another source of information on salaries for scientists and engineers is the National Science Foundation. All NSF reports are available free of charge on the World Wide Web. The salary reports published by the Science Resources Studies Division are published annually and contain much valuable information about employment trends. According to the NSF, the employment of scientists and engineers reached 3.2 million in 1995. Engineers represented 42 percent, or 1.34 million of the employed scientists and engineers. Of these, 357,000 engineers were employed in the subfield of electrical engineering.

There are very substantial differences among workers in the same field, depending on level of education and years of experience. In 1995, the median annual salary for scientists and engineers with bachelor's degrees was $48,000. For those with master's degrees, the median annual salary was $53,000; for doctorate holders, $58,000. Engineers are at the higher end of the scale, earning more than computer and mathematical scientists.

You can expect your wages to rise steadily the longer you are employed. For example, people who earned their bachelor's or master's degrees in the early 1980s were earning on average about $15,000 more than those who graduated in 1995, as they had seniority.

Don't forget the "business" side of lasers as you consider opportunities in laser technology. Companies offering lasers need product sales and support staff—knowledgeable men and women who can talk to customers about their needs and can make recommendations that may ultimately result in a sale. Backgrounds useful for obtaining those positions will probably include marketing and sales training, as well as enough science and technology to understand customer problems and the products being offered.

CHAPTER 10

WOMEN AND MINORITIES

There's good news and bad news about opportunities for women and minorities who want to work with laser technology. The good news is that sex and ethnic origin are no barriers to qualified candidates. In other words, if you have the prerequisite skills and desire you have excellent chances of finding employment—if (and it's a big if) companies are hiring. The bad news is that women, Blacks, Hispanics, and Native Americans are still underrepresented in undergraduate and graduate science and engineering programs. In undergraduate and graduate enrollments the share of total enrollments by Asian Americans continue to rise, particularly among men.

ENROLLMENT STATISTICS

Between 1985 and 1995, the number of students enrolled in undergraduate and graduate programs in engineering and science rose by 18 percent. One of the reasons for this increase is that women, minorities, and people with disabilities began entering science and engineering in higher numbers. Where there was once a significant gender gap in high school mathematics performance, by 1998 that difference had largely disappeared. And for the first time women were earning close to half of the undergraduate degrees being awarded in science and engineering. That said, there are still some discrepancies. For example, while women earned about 50 percent of the bachelor's degrees in biological and agricultural sciences, they earned only about 30 percent of the degrees in physical sciences and mathematical/computer sciences. And in engineering women made up only about 17 percent of those graduating with a B.S. As might be expected, the lower rate of women in engineering programs continues through graduate school.

Although women constitute 46 percent of the U.S. labor force, they only account for 22 percent of all those employed in science and engineering. This is largely due to the fact that only more recently have women been entering these fields.

Among minority groups, Blacks, Hispanics, and Native Americans are far less likely to be enrolled in institutions of higher education. Although these groups constitute 23 percent of the U.S. population, they make up only about 13 percent of all undergraduate students enrolled in science and engineering programs. The good news is that the college enrollment for minorities has been steadily increasing since 1990. By 1995, Blacks earned 7 percent of science and engineering bachelor's degrees, Hispanics made up another 6 percent of graduates, and Native Americans earned 0.6 percent. These numbers are still dismayingly low, and as a result only 6 percent of those employed in science and engineering are from these underrepresented minority groups.

In contrast, Asians constitute a well-represented minority group. Although Asians make up only about 3.4 percent of the U.S. resident population, they account for 10 percent of the total labor force in science and engineering.

Minority women also are better represented in science and engineering than in other categories. Black women are far more likely to earn a bachelor's degree than Black men. In 1995, Black women were awarded 4.3 percent of the undergraduate degrees in science and engineering; by contrast, Black men received only 2.6 percent.

However, the numbers of Black men and women receiving advanced degrees in these fields are comparable, with Black men receiving only 1.5 percent of the doctoral degrees, and Black women only 1.4 percent.

Current data and historical trends related to the education of women and minorities in the sciences is compiled by the National Science Foundation. A detailed report by the NSF Division of Science Resources Studies, entitled "Women, Minorities, and Persons with Disabilities in Science and Engineering: 1998," is available on-line at www.nsf.org. You also can receive information about this report, as well as about many other education and labor force surveys, by writing to the National Science Foundation, Division of Science Resources Studies, 4201 Wilson Boulevard, Suite 965, Arlington, Virginia, 22230.

CONCENTRATE ON SCIENCE AND MATH

If you are a woman or a member of a minority group, what can you do to become qualified to work with lasers? One important strategy is to excel in science and mathematics. As a junior high or high school student, sign up for all the math and science possible. Often, especially in large metropolitan areas such as Chicago or Atlanta, there are opportunities for enrichment programs in those subjects. Even if such programs require your after-school, weekend, or vacation time, take advantage of everything you can. The skills you gain and the contacts you make can be invaluable. Also, as you begin to read about schools with engineering or optics programs, write to the director of admissions at those institutions that interest you. Ask about summer studies, minority recruitment, or special programs you can join.

Statistics from the National Research Council indicate that the mathematics achievement of the top 5 percent of the twelfth grade students is lower in the United States than in other industrialized nations. The average twelfth grade mathematics student in Japan outperforms 95 percent of comparable U.S. twelfth graders.

Math and science are two important tools you'll need to qualify for jobs working with lasers. Optics and electro-optics are demanding, "hard" sciences. Finding opportunities for additional study and taking advantage of them may give you the edge you need for admission to a top-quality college or university program.

SOCIETY OF WOMEN ENGINEERS

The Society of Women Engineers is an organization dedicated to helping women who choose to pursue careers in engineering. The society also tracks the achievements and statistics of women in this field and sponsors numerous educational programs (including a unique e-mail mentoring program) and more than ninety scholarships. These scholarships range in amount from $200 to over $5,000 a year and are open only to women who are majoring in engineering or computer science. To receive information about the scholarships, send a self-addressed envelope to Society of Women Engineers Headquarters, 120 Wall Street, 11th Floor, New York, NY, 10005-3902. You also can write to the SWE for information on joining one of the local student chapters, which are located throughout the United States.

The web site for the SWE, which can be found on-line at www.swe.org, is an excellent resource for women of all ages who are considering pursuing a career in engineering. Among the many resources you will find are Career Guidance Tools, which will help you choose the best science curriculum for your plan of study.

AMERICAN COUNCIL ON EDUCATION

Another educational organization that collects and publishes information on education is the American Council on Education (ACE). In 1987, ACE launched its Minority Initiative in response to declining rates of minority participation in higher education. The Office of Minorities in Higher Education (OMHE), which is part of ACE, is a major source of information on the education status of minorities. Through OMHE you also can learn about those programs that serve underrepresented minority students. Every other year the OMHE sponsors an important national conference on diversity and improving minority participation in postsecondary education, called "Educating All of One Nation."

To find out more about the OMHE, write to Office of Minorities in Higher Education, American Council on Education, One Dupont Circle NW, Washington, DC 20036. You can visit the ACE web site at www.acenet.edu, where you will find information on minority programs as well as programs for women.

CHAPTER 11

INTERNATIONAL OPPORTUNITIES

LASER TECHNOLOGY IN CANADA

Lasers and related technology are beginning to play a more important part in Canadian employment. Research is continuing at a number of locations, including at the Ontario Hydro Services Company. There, various applications of lasers are studied, including the use of lasers for induced chemical reactions for isotope separation. Lasers and fiber optic sensors for measuring temperatures of generators are also being studied.

At the University of Toronto, several noted professors are involved with research in lasers and related topics. Chemistry professor Dr. Geraldine Kenny-Wallace, Nobel prize–winner Dr. John Polanyi, and Dr. Boris Stoicheff, a renowned physicist, are among them.

At Photonics Research Ontario (PRO) researchers are developing advanced laser systems that will provide high-power lasers covering the ultraviolet and infrared ranges. These lasers will leave industrial applications as well as be useful in research programs.

Other research underway at PRO involves optical diagnostics as well as the use of lasers in measurement.

For more information, write to Photonics Research Ontario, 60 St. George Street, Suite 129, Toronto, Ontario, Canada M5S 1A7. The web site is www.pro.on.ca.

Alberta Laser Centre

At the University of Alberta, research in laser technology has been pursued since the mid-1960s. The Alberta Laser Institute, established in 1984, fostered research in various laser applications, concentrating on industrial applications, but current programs involve robotics, materials processing, laser sensors, electronics, and medical applications. Facilities include state-of-the-art CAD/CAM-based laser manufacturing capabilities that include cutting, heat treating, cladding, welding, and drilling—processes that are used on materials as diverse as ceramics, plastics, rubbers, glass, wood, textiles, paper, and electronic circuit fabrication elements.

Laser research is currently being conducted under the aegis of the program of Condensed Matter Physics. You can find out more by writing the program, which is part of the Department of Physics, 412 Avadh Bhatia Physics Laboratory, University of Alberta, Edmonton, Alberta, Canada T6G 2J1; (780) 492-5286. The web site address is www.phys.ualberta.ca.

For additional information, contact the Alberta Laser Institute, 9924 Forty-fifth Avenue, Edmonton, Alberta, Canada T63 5J1.

LASER TECHNOLOGY IN BRITAIN

Opportunities for careers in laser technology in Britain are similar to those in the United States. For instance, lasers are used in manufacturing, surgery, communications, defense applications, and metrology (the science of measurement). "New uses are being found all the time," says Charles Childes, divisional secretary, Electronic Engineering Associates.

One British firm, Laser Scientific Services Ltd., in Cambridgeshire, England, has successfully developed the technology for laser cutting large aluminum aircraft panels in three dimensions. Technicians at the factory operate computer-programmed lasers to cut out the central slots and outer profile of a panel for a strategic aircraft.

Because of the laser's ability to produce a clean, sharp cut, the high quality cut edge of the panels needs no further machining and only limited deburring. For flat sheet work, tooling is not normally required. Complex geometric shapes can be cut in panels of various materials, using a sophisticated digitizer and computer-aided program system with direct numerical control. The thickness that can be cut depends on the material and the laser power.

Laser Scientific Services Ltd., which sells, installs, and maintains industrial laser systems, also uses a computer numerically controlled (CNC) laser to cut out lettering or logos with precise repeatability. Because the laser generates little heat, there is no distortion. A wide range of plastic, metal, laminate, and composite materials can be used. Other activities of the company include cutting, profiling, scribing, or drilling of ceramic components for the microelectronics industry. The company has set up a joint venture operation, using laser technology, in Denmark.

Addresses

For further information on lasers in the U.K., contact:

Electric Engineering Associates
    Leicester House
    8 Leicester Street
    London WC2H 7BN
    England
    (0171 437 0678)

British Medical Association
  British Medical Association House
  Tavistock Square
  London WCI 9JP
  England
  (0171 387 4499)

LASER TECHNOLOGY IN AUSTRALIA

Australia has a strong background of research and development in mining, biomedical sciences, and scientific instrumentations—a background that is reflected in a high level of laser R&D, applications, and manufacturing.

One key center for laser research and development has been established at Macquarie University in New South Wales. Here, under the direction of Professor Jim Piper, a laser physicist, researchers plan to investigate the basic science of laser physics while tailoring technology to specific applications and manufacturing within Australia. The center also plans to emphasize medical applications of lasers, both for therapeutic diagnostics and for surgery. Manufacturing products arising from the center are fabricated by Metalaser.

Australia currently is focusing its laser efforts in two fields: materials processing and medical lasers. Many of the industrial lasers are integrated with computer numerically controlled (CNC) systems, so skills in computer programming are helpful. Medical lasers range from CO_2 lasers that are effectively miniaturized (a nine-centimeter laser puts out about ninety watts of power) to metal vapor lasers, developed in Australia. Copper and gold vapor lasers have been marketed; lasers using other metals are being tested. One joint project with Monash University and the University of Colorado in the United States involves a metal vapor laser that operates at room temperature, regarded as useful for biotechnology or biomedical processing instrumentation.

Nd:YAG lasers are being developed for ophthalmology use by Laserex, an Australian company with some forty employees. Physicians at major hospitals and medical centers are using various types of lasers for dermatology, cancer surgery, gynecology, and photodynamic laser therapy.

Training Opportunities

Government officials continue to review the state of lasers in Australia. In the late 1980s an important meeting was held to determine the strategy for Victoria, according to Dr. Alan J. Jones, assistant director, Exploitable Science and Technology, Department of Industry, Technology, and Commerce. "We have a shortage of skills," Jones says, "especially in the area of service and maintenance of existing laser systems. We're looking for qualified technical people."

It was determined at the time that Australians needed more technical training. "University graduates have insufficient laser hands-on experience, and Ph.D. graduates would find no job satisfaction in intermittent repairs of equipment," Jones says. "There is an identifiable need for laser technologists who could gain their skills by one- to two-year associations with existing laser R&D facilities."

Both Jones and Dr. George L. Paul, director of the Centre for Industrial Laser Applications, School of Physics, the University of New South Wales, stress the need for more course work in lasers. At the University of New South Wales, training in lasers and optics is offered in the third year of physics training. Other universities offer postgraduate courses related to lasers. A center for laser physics also operates at the Australian National University, Canberra, with a focus on mechanisms of laser fusion. Conventional Nd:YAG performance has been considerably improved during the course of this work, and this has found its way into the products of a new company, Electro-Optic Systems, which won a large contract from the United States DOD for a series of its laser radar systems.

Research by postgraduate students also is being done at a number of other universities, according to Paul. However, he says, there aren't too many courses on modern optics being offered in Australia.

Some laser companies, Paul feels, believe it is better to retrain existing employees to use lasers than to hire specially trained technicians. "For instance, Laser Lab in Melbourne is successfully coupling U.S.-based lasers interfaced to up to five-axis computer numerical controlled specialized cutting systems. The CNC software is designed by the Australian Numerical Control Association. Laser Lab, which supplies lasers for cutting, uses people they pulled from the factory floor and trained to use lasers," he explains.

"If young people want to work with lasers, then there may be job opportunities with similar companies. For instance, Metalaser, which is in an expansion phase after purchasing Photon Sources, a California-based firm, is looking for more people."

Paul suggests that persons with training in optics who would like to get into the scientific instrument market are likely to find jobs. "There certainly are opportunities for trained people who come out to Australia," he explains.

It's a World Market

Paul emphasizes that from the Australian viewpoint, the laser market has become worldwide. "For those who want to get into new and exciting technologies, there are opportunities for vast profits," he says. "Teams of creative people are needed—people of diverse backgrounds, like chemists, physicists, metallurgists.

Solving problems involves a wide range of skills, and that can be stimulating!"

Paul also points out that lasers, like some other technical fields in Australia, present niche market opportunities. "There are a number of these areas that Australian companies have identified and in which they're doing very well," he says. "For instance, Laser Lab in Melbourne is successful in using lasers for cutting. Laserex, another company, produces high-quality pocket-sized laser pointers. They supply about 50 percent of the world market, and they're doing extremely well. And Metalaser is doing a successful job in niche marketing for medical applications of metal vapor lasers."

Although there's been some shakeout in laser companies, Paul says, he thinks the bigger companies are getting bigger. "Perhaps in the future, there will only be a small number of major laser companies," he says. "But it's my belief that there are many areas of laser applications that have yet to be defined."

Additional Information

For more information on lasers and laser training in Australia, contact:

Centre for Lasers and Applications
   Macquarie University
   North Ryde
   New South Wales 2113
   Australia
   (02 805-7911)

Centre for Industrial Laser Applications
   University of New South Wales
   Kensington, NSW 2033
   Australia
   (02 697-4586)

Footscray Institute of Technology
  P.O. Box 64, Ballarat Road
  Footscray, Victoria 3011
  Australia
  (03 688-4277)

University of Queensland
  Director, Laser Applications Laboratory
  St. Lucia, Queensland 4067
  Australia
  (07 377-2637)

Exploitable Science and Technology
  Department of Industry, Technology, and Commerce
  51 Allara Street
  Canberra City 2600
  Australia

ASSOCIATIONS

Because laser technology spans many areas, there are a number of trade associations involved with its varying aspects. Some of them have significant reduction in membership rates for qualified students. Most associations sponsor conferences or meetings that students can attend for reduced fees. Nearly all associations have journals, magazines, or other publications, and often these are available to students at discount rates. Some associations offer career guidance information. In addition, several associations offer videotapes that can be borrowed or rented.

There are many advantages to joining a professional association while you are still in school. Frequently local or regional chapters have monthly meetings that student members can attend. These gatherings give you a chance to talk with established professionals, as well as those just beginning careers. The friendships you make will be extremely important.

Serving on a committee of such an association or society, even though you may still be a student, is well worth your time and effort. The informal contact with members, the chance to truly be a participant instead of just a spectator, the behind-scenes awareness of how a meeting or conference is actually put together—all these are good learning experiences. So is the chance to demonstrate leadership ability. While your motive for participation should be based on your genuine interest in the organization, nevertheless your activities will be watched by those already working in the field. They can help you with career questions and be a valuable source of information.

American Society for Laser Medicine and Surgery

This professional association of more than three thousand members in the United States and twenty additional countries is dedicated to facilitating exchange of information concerning medical applications of lasers. Members include physicists who develop devices, biomedical engineers who adapt them for practical purposes, safety officers who supervise workings of lasers, biologists who study the effects of laser energy on living tissue, and health professionals who treat patients with lasers.

Founded in 1980 the ASLMS has several classes of members. The Fellowship category includes scientists, physicians, physicists, veterinarians, podiatrists, dentists, and nurse-scientists. The Member category includes health care professionals, such as physical therapists, biomedical engineers, hospital administrators, and clinical nurses not eligible for Fellow status. Commercial Fellows are members involved in the commercial aspect of lasers as related to medicine, including development and marketing.

Listed by the American Medical Association as one of its recognized medical societies, ASLMS has formulated standards and guidelines for establishing safe, effective laser programs in hospitals and other institutions and has recommended standards for those who conduct both basic and advanced courses. ASLMS attempts to keep its membership informed about all postgraduate courses and training programs in laser biology, nursing, medicine, and surgery.

In association with other national, regional, international, and specialty laser societies, the ASLMS cooperates with the International Congress of Lasers in Surgery and Medicine, the Laser Institute of America, and the Society of Photo-Optical Instrumentation Engineers (SPIE) in organizing programs.

Lasers in Surgery and Medicine is the official journal of the American Society for Laser Medicine and Surgery. It carries proceedings of annual scientific meetings. A bimonthly newsletter includes news items, a calendar of events, courses and programs, and updates on government and insurance policies relating to laser biology, medicine, and surgery. The newsletter also includes a career opportunities section for job-seekers and employers.

For more information, write or call American Society for Laser Medicine and Surgery, 2404 Stewart Square, Wausau, WI 54401, (715) 845-9283. The web site is www.aslms.org.

Institute of Industrial Engineers

The Institute of Industrial Engineers (IIE) is a major international professional society concerned with the design, improvement, and installation of systems for industrial engineering. Members are concerned with the design, improvement, and installation of integrated systems of people, material, information, equipment, and energy—all the elements in the "productivity" equation.

IIE's twenty-four thousand members belong to one or more of twenty-three separate divisions. Each division publishes newsletters that keep members up to date on new ideas and new developments in the field.

The institute has more than 325 local groups worldwide, plus over 100 university chapters at most universities offering industrial engineering curricula. All members receive *Industrial Engineering,* the monthly magazine. Books, periodicals, and software also are offered at membership discounts.

Two major conferences yearly (the Annual International Industrial Engineering Conference and Show and the Fall Industrial

Engineering Conference), plus numerous seminars, continuing education programs, and workshops help members keep up with what's new professionally.

Through its career guidance program, which takes place primarily at the local level through established chapters, IIE acquaints thousands of young people each year with the opportunities and advantages of a career in industrial engineering. Through scholarships and fellowships, IIE rewards outstanding student members for scholastic excellence on both the graduate and the undergraduate levels.

For information on IIE, write or call Institute of Industrial Engineers, 25 Technology Park/Atlanta, Norcross, GA 30092, (770) 449-0460. Their web site is www.iienet.org.

Laser Institute of America

Founded in 1968, the Laser Institute of America (LIA) is a nonprofit professional society of seventeen hundred members for the advancement and promotion of laser technology and applications. It conducts continuing education courses, seminars, and technical symposia and offers a variety of educational materials and publications. The Laser Institute publishes the *Journal of Laser Applications, Laser Safety Guide,* and *LIA Today.*

Within the institute, members have the opportunity to indicate their principal area of interest, choosing among medicine and biology; materials processing; inspection, measurement, and control; optical communications; information processing; holography; safety; scientific applications; imaging and display technology; and photochemistry/spectroscopy.

Student chapters have been formed at a number of colleges, universities, and technical institutes. These chapters work closely with professionals.

LIA sponsors one of the major annual conferences on lasers—ICALEO, the International Congress on Applications of Lasers and Electro-Optics—in cooperation with the American Society for Laser Medicine and Surgery; the Society of Manufacturing Engineers; the International Society of Podiatric Laser Surgery; the American Society of Metals, International; the Midwest Bio-Laser Institute; the High Temperature Society of Japan; the Western Institute for Laser Treatment; the Japan Laser Processing Society; the Japan Society for Laser Technology; and IFS Conferences, Ltd.

ICALEO features four simultaneous technical conferences: Laser Materials Processing, Laser Research in Medicine, Optical Methods in Flow and Particle Diagnostics, and Electro-Optic Sensing and Measurement.

Throughout the year LIA works closely with other laser-related organizations to coordinate various short courses for professionals. Its laser electro-optics offerings include "Fundamentals and Applications of Lasers"; "Modern Experimental Spectroscopy"; "Laser Safety"; "Hazards, Inspection and Control"; "Advanced Industrial Laser Safety Officer Training"; and "Medical Laser Safety Officers Training." These three- or four-day courses are offered at various locations around the country.

For information on LIA, including the location of student chapters, write or call Laser Institute of America, 5151 Monroe Street, Toledo, OH 43623, (419) 882-8706. The web site in www.laserinstitute.org.

Optical Society of America

Founded in 1916, the Optical Society of America has more than twelve thousand individual members, including scientists, engineers, and technicians from the United States and fifty other countries. Members work in industry, educational institutions, and government agencies, and include a number of Nobel laureates.

More than sixty companies with an interest in optics have pledged corporate support to the mission statement of the OSA: "To increase and diffuse the knowledge of optics, to promote the common interests of investigators of optical problems, of designers and users of optical apparatus of all kinds, and to encourage cooperation among them."

Among OSA publications are its peer-reviewed journals and its news magazine, *Optics and Photonics News*. Each is devoted to a specific aspect of optical science or techology. They are *Applied Optics, Journal of Lightwave Technology, Journal of the Optical Society of America A: Optics and Image Science, Journal of the Optical Society of America B: Optical Physics, Journal of Optical Technology,* and *Optics Letters*.

In addition, OSA publishes translated journals in English: *Chinese Physics—Lasers, Optics and Spectroscopy,* and *Soviet Journal of Optical Technology*.

Information on lasers and laser physics is generally found in *JOSA B* and in *Applied Optics*. Information on topics such as fiber and cable technologies is covered in *Journal of Lightwave Technology*, published jointly by OSA and the Institute of Electrical and Electronics Engineers. This publication presents advances in the science, technology, and engineering of optical guided waves. *Optics and Photonics News* includes ongoing coverage of developments in instrumentation and systems applications for lasers and optical fibers. *Optics Letters* includes new results in optics research, including fiber-optics technology.

More than twenty digests are published annually by OSA. These cover all OSA-sponsored and cosponsored conferences and meetings.

Although OSA does not sponsor student chapters at universities, individual students can join the society at a reduced rate of $18 per year. Student membership entitles persons to discounts on all publications and journals. In addition, students who are members can attend all OSA-sponsored conferences at reduced rates. If they wish, they can be put in touch with local OSA chapters and can attend local meetings.

For additional information on the Optical Society of America, write or call its executive office, 2010 Massachusetts Avenue NW, Washington, DC 20036, (202) 223-8130. The web site is www. osa.org.

Society of Manufacturing Engineers

The Society of Manufacturing Engineers (SME) is one of the largest professional engineering associations in the world, with more than sixty thousand members with 275 chapters, districts, and regions worldwide. It has more than ten thousand student members and more than 240 student chapters.

Within SME, various associations are concerned with different aspects of manufacturing: Robotics International (RI/SME), Computer & Automated Systems Association (CASA/SME), Association for Finishing Processes (AFP/SME), North American Manufacturing Research Institute (NAMRI/SME), and Machine Vision Association (MVA/SME).

As the umbrella organization for these associations, SME annually sponsors more than 150 special programs, 50 technical conferences, 40 expositions, and 500 symposia and workshops. It publishes technical papers on various subjects that can be purchased either individually or (often) in various collections. An online electronic database search, available through the society's library service, allows members and nonmembers to access papers on desired topics quickly.

SME has a Laser Council, composed of individuals experienced in the use of lasers in manufacturing. Meeting several times throughout the year, the Laser Council plans SPOT, an intensive annual conference that features papers describing laser technology and applications.

For more information on SME, write or call the Society of Manufacturing Engineers, One SME Drive, P.O. Box 930, Dearborn, MI 48121-0930, (313) 271-1500. Membership rates include a subscription to *Manufacturing Engineering,* SME's monthly magazine. The web site is www.sme.org.

International Society of Optical Engineering (SPIE)

Founded in 1955 and formerly called the Society of Photo-Optical Instrumentation Engineers, SPIE has changed its name but kept its initials and its mission. SPIE is a nonprofit society dedicated to advancing engineering and scientific applications of optical, electro-optical, and opto-electronic instrumentation, systems, and technology. Its 11,500 members include scientists, engineers, and users interested in these technologies. SPIE uses publications and conferences to communicate new developments and applications to the scientific, engineering, and user communities.

SPIE sponsors a number of conferences on many topics. Typical of conferences related to lasers is SPIE's O-E/LASE, a weeklong conference covering opto-electronics and laser applications in science and engineering. Separate symposia are held on Lasers and Optics; Innovative Science & Technology, with related conferences on Optical Signal Processing; Laser Spectroscopy—Techniques, Applications, Data Bases, and Equipment; Medical Applications of Lasers, Fiber Optics, and Electro-Optics; and Electronic Imaging and Optical Mass Data Storage.

At SPIE conferences, exhibitors demonstrate products, instruments, and services used in optics, lasers, imaging, spectroscopy, interferometry, optical mass data storage, optical signal processing, and medicine.

For further information on joining SPIE or on its conferences and publications, write SPIE—The International Society for Optical Engineering, P.O. Box 10, Bellingham, WA 98227-0010, (206) 676-3290.

APPENDIX B

RECOMMENDED READING AND RESOURCES

Laser technology is developing so rapidly that you will want to keep up with news and developments. The reference collections at your local public or college library can provide you with basic information on the history, theory, and uses of laser technology. To stay on top of current developments, you will want to read the professional and scientific publications that cover new discoveries and applications. And you also will find that using the Internet as a reference tool will provide you with access to many materials that you would not otherwise be able to obtain.

Periodicals

Many of the periodicals listed here will be too specialized to be found in most public libraries; however, they may be included in the holdings of local colleges or universities, or they can be obtained through interlibrary loan. Speak with your reference librarian to find out how to request materials from affiliated libraries if your library does not subscribe to the particular journal or magazine that you want to read. One way to get up-to-date information is to use library indexes. You've probably already used *Reader's Guide to Periodical Literature,* an index commonly found in public libraries that tracks articles in many popular magazines by subject matter. Although *Reader's Guide to Periodical Literature* is a good place to start, the material referred to may not be technical enough for your needs.

Fortunately, most libraries have companion indexes, organized along similar lines. *Business Periodicals Index* is a similar reference work that focuses on magazines and publications of interest in financial and economic fields. You can look up "lasers" in recent volumes of BPI and then go to the individual publications for particular articles. Stories and news you would find about lasers might include material on company profits, mergers and acquisitions, lawsuits, or future sales.

Another good way in which you can keep up with technical advances in laser technology is to use *Applied Science and Technology Index,* another specialized index available at most libraries. Here, the broad topic of "lasers" is subdivided into such headings as "lasers—industrial applications," "laser printers," or "lasers—measurement methods."

At the beginning of a bound volume of each of these indexes you will find a list of the periodicals covered by that particular index along with an address and subscription rate for each. You will find that certain publications show up frequently in these indexes. If your library does not subscribe to a magazine you wish, you may want to write the publisher directly, enclosing money and a large, self-addressed, stamped envelope for a recent copy. Looking closely at the magazine can help you decide whether you may want to become a subscriber or whether you want to ask your library for help in locating more copies.

In large metropolitan areas such as Chicago, many corporations and research laboratories maintain their own libraries on topics of interest in their particular field. You will find special books and magazines on food and nutrition, for example, at the Quaker Oats

Research Laboratories in suburban Barrington, Illinois, while Kemper Insurance Company in suburban Long Grove, Illinois, has a collection that includes *Best Insurance Reports,* the *West Reporter System* (law digests), a collection on alcoholism, and various proceedings and transactions of societies and conferences. Kemper's subject strengths are insurance and insurance law, law in general, and management.

If you are located in an area that has companies that manufacture, sell, or service equipment in electronics, physics, or telecommunications, those businesses, especially if they are large, may well have corporate libraries. Your own public library reference librarian will know what's available in your area, whether you can use those corporate libraries for study and reading, and whom to call at a particular location to find out what periodicals and books they have. Often if a magazine is expensive or so specialized that a public library doesn't subscribe to it, these corporations will have copies you can look at.

Many libraries in large metropolitan areas also have a service under which they share information. A number of public libraries belong to Central Serials Service, an interlibrary consortium that makes photocopies of articles you can't find at your local library and sends them to your local librarian—at no charge to you. There are a number of rules you must obey to use this service; most of them have to do with the frequency with which you want articles from a particular publication. Copyright laws permit limited reproduction of copyrighted material, so librarians want to be sure you do not ask for more than you're entitled to.

Still another way in which you may get material on lasers is through computer searching. Reference librarians often are tied in with various databases. Because you are a cardholder at your local library, the library may be willing to do a certain number of free or low-cost searches per year on topics related to lasers. If you are requesting an on-line search, check first with your librarian to see whether you will be charged. Generally, you can probably find more than enough material in your field of interest by reading copies of the publications listed below.

American Journal of Physics
Applied Optics
Applied Physics
Fiber and Integrated Optics
IEEE Journal of Quantum Electronics
IEEE Photonics Technology
Industrial Laser Review
Journal of Applied Physics
Journal of Biomedical Optics
Journal of Laser Applications
Journal of Nonlinear Optical Physics and Materials
Journal of Soviet Laser Research
Laser Chemistry
Laser and Electro-Optic Reviews
Lasers in Engineering
Laser Focus World
Lasers and Optronics
Laser and Particle Beams
Laser Physics
Medical Laser Insight
Optical Engineering
Optical and Quantum Electronics
Optics Communications
Optics and Laser Technology
Optics and Lasers in Engineering
Optics Letters
Optics and Spectroscopy
Physical Review

Books

In order to increase your understanding of how lasers work and of laser applications in various fields, it will be helpful for you to do as much reading as possible. If books suggested below are not available through your school or public library, a librarian can probably arrange to borrow them through interlibrary loan.

The reading level and complexity of ideas explored in the books on this list vary considerably—that is, you cannot necessarily tell from a book's title just how difficult it will be. One good way to be sure you understand basic principles of lasers is to begin reading at a level slightly below your present knowledge of physics, optics, or electronics. There are several books that describe laser projects that you can do in your home or in a science classroom. These books provide important safety guidelines that will allow laser enthusiasts to experiment without risking harm to themselves.

Because knowledge about lasers and laser applications is growing rapidly, as you progress in your self-study beyond understanding the basic technology, you will want to pay attention to publication dates, so that the information you obtain is as current as possible. That is why keeping up with trade journals and magazine articles is also essential.

The following list is, of course, by no means complete. Your reference librarian can help you find other books about lasers that you may enjoy. You may want to consult your math or science teacher or even your school district's curriculum consultant in science. Another way you can find more books is to write to one of the colleges or universities listed in Chapter 8. Address your letter to the dean of the engineering school, the head of the physics department, or to someone holding a comparable position. Tell them you would like to know more about lasers and ask them to recommend a reading list for high school students.

By the time you've sampled eight or ten books from the list below, you should know how serious you are about working with lasers. Like many people, you will find the story of laser light and its applications fascinating and challenging!

Barrett, N. S. *Lasers and Holograms.* London, England: Franklin Watts, 1985.

Bender, Lionel. *Lasers in Action.* New York: The Bookwright Press, 1985.

Billings, Charlene W. *Lasers—The New Technology of Light.* New York: Facts on File, Inc., 1992.

Bromberg, Joan Lisa. *The Laser in America, 1950–1970.* Cambridge, MA: The MIT Press, 1991.

Brown, Ronald. *Lasers: Tools of Modern Technology.* Garden City, NY: Doubleday & Company, Inc., 1968.

Burroughs, William. *Lasers.* New York: Warwick Press, 1982.

Gibilisco, Stan. *Understanding Lasers.* Blue Ridge Summit, PA: TAB Books, Inc., 1989.

Hallmark, Clayton L. and Delton T. Horn. *Lasers, the Light Fantastic.* Blue Ridge Summit, PA: TAB Books, Inc., 1987.

Harbison, James P. *Lasers: Harnessing the Atom's Light.* New York: Scientific American Library, 1998.

Hecht, Jeff. *The Laser Guidebook,* 2nd Edition. Blue Ridge Summit, PA: TAB Books, 1992.

———. *Understanding Lasers.* Howard W. Sams & Company, 1988.

Hecht, Jeff and Dick Teresi. *Laser: Super Tool of the 1980s.* New Haven, CT and New York: Ticknor and Fields, 1982.

Hitz, C. Breck. *Understanding Laser Technology: An Intuitive Introduction to Basic and Advanced Laser Concepts.* Tulsa, OK: PennWell Books, 1985.

Horn, Delton T. *Laser Experimenter's Handbook,* 2nd Edition. Blue Ridge Summit, PA: TAB Books, 1988.

Iannini, Robert E. *Build Your Own Laser, Phaser, Ion Ray Gun & Other Working Space-Age Projects.* Blue Ridge Summit, PA: TAB Books, 1983.

———. *Build Your Own Working Fiberoptic, Infrared, & Laser Space-Age Projects.* Blue Ridge Summit, PA: TAB Books, 1987.

Iovine, John. *Homemade Holograms: The Complete Guide to Inexpensive, Do-It-Yourself Holography.* Blue Ridge Summit, PA: TAB Books, 1990.

Kettlekamp, Larry. *Lasers, the Miracle Light.* New York: William Morrow and Company, 1979.

Kock, Winston K. *Lasers and Holography: An Introduction to Coherent Optics.* Garden City, NY: Doubleday & Company, Inc., 1969.

Kuhn, Kelin J. *Laser Engineering.* New York: Prentice Hall, 1998.

Laurence, Clifford L. *The Laser Book: A New Technology of Light.* New York: Prentice Hall Press, 1986.

Lenk, John D. *Lenk's Laser Handbook: Featuring CD, CDV, and CD-ROM Technology.* New York: McGraw-Hill, 1992.

McAleese, Frank G. *The Laser Experimenter's Handbook.* Blue Ridge Summit, PA: TAB Books, Inc., 1979.

McComb, Gordon. *The Laser Cookbook: 88 Practical Projects.* Blue Ridge Summit, PA: TAB Books, Inc., 1988.

———. *Lasers, Ray Guns, & Light Cannons: Projects from the Wizard's Workbench.* Blue Ridge Summit, PA: McGraw Hill, 1997.

Mims, Forrest M., III. *Lasers (The Incredible Light Machine).* New York: David McKay Company, Inc., 1977.

Safford, Edward L., Jr. *The Fiberoptics and Laser Handbook.* Blue Ridge Summit, PA: TAB Books, Inc., 1984.

Schneider, Herman. *Laser Light.* New York: McGraw-Hill Book Company, 1978.

Siegman, A. E. *Lasers.* Mill Valley, CA: University Science Books, 1986.

Silfvast, William T. *Laser Fundamentals.* Cambridge, England: Cambridge University Press, 1996.

Stehling, Kurt R. *Lasers and their Applications.* Cleveland and New York: The World Publishing Company, 1966.

Svelto, Orazio (Editor), David C. Hanna (Translator). *Principles of Lasers,* 4th Edition. New York: Plenum Publishing Corporation, 1998.

Unterseher, Fred, Jeannene Hansen, and Bob Schlesinger. *The Holography Handbook.* Berkeley, CA: Ross Books, 1993.

Verdeyen, Joseph T. *Laser Electronics,* third edition. New York: Prentice Hall, 1994.

Wenyon, Michael. *Understanding Holography.* New York: Arco
  Publishing, Inc., 1985.
Wilson, J., and J. F. B. Hawkes. *Lasers, Principles and Applications.* New
  York: Prentice Hall, 1987.

Using the Internet

The World Wide Web is a tremendous resource for researching
the science and applications of lasers. You can access the web
pages of various organizations and institutions to discover what
research projects are currently underway at their facilities. Frequently they also will provide links to other organizations involved
in lasers, optics, or physics. Follow the links from more established
institutions before you try a global search using one of the major
search engines, such as Yahoo! or Alta Vista. When the "webmas-
ter" at institutions such as Livermore is creating links to other laser
sites, he or she will often weed out those that carry inaccurate or
out-of-date information. Let the experts serve as your guide, as you
will find that there is so much information on-line, that a general
search through the Internet may overwhelm you.

Another interesting way of finding out about lasers is to read
laser-related USENET Newsgroups. USENET Newsgroups are
like public bulletin boards. People who are interested in a particular topic sign up to read e-mail "postings" about the specific subject. There are more than twenty-thousand active newsgroups in
the United States alone, several of which deal with lasers. (At the
time of publication, two active groups are "alt.lasers" and
"sci.optics." Your Internet Service Provider can give you the information on how to search for newsgroups; the software for reading
these postings is included with your Internet access software, such
as the web browser or your e-mail application.)

If you decide to join a USENET discussion group, make sure
you follow the proper "netiquette." Read postings for a while

before you write your own, so that you can get a sense for the types of questions that are appropriate. Many discussion groups will have an FAQ (Frequently Asked Questions) document that may hold the answer to your question.